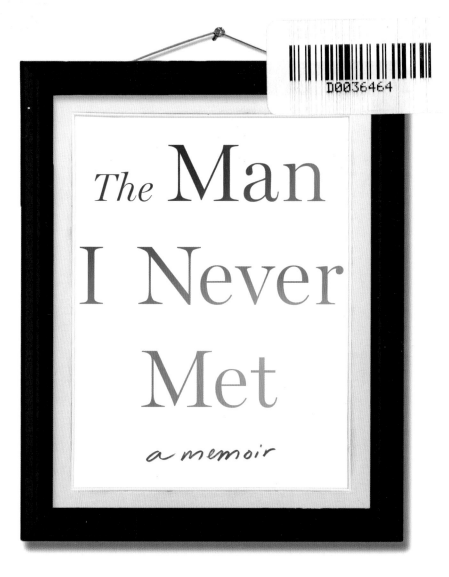

The Man
I Never
Met

a memoir

Adam Schefter

Praise for *The Man I Never Met*

"Schefter's book is affecting not only for the story it tells of how the author learned to honor his wife's husband as 'the fifth member of [his] family,' but also for how it shows a man growing into a mature understanding of the true meaning of love and sacrifice. An unexpectedly moving memoir." —*Kirkus Reviews*

"Schefter successfully communicates his joy in finding love and family, and in a friendship with a man he never knew."
—*Publishers Weekly*

"Part character study, part examination of what can be gained through loss. And it's all heart and hope, a captivating and deeply personal tale about the transformative power of love."
—Associated Press

"Every good life makes its foundation on a bedrock of gratitude. This is a story that draws out the fundamentals of good living and makes you glad to be alive."
—Kelly Corrigan, bestselling author of
The Middle Place and *Glitter and Glue*

"A brave, inspiring story of two men with different fates, never meeting, yet proving the connectivity of life through the overwhelming power of love."
—Mitch Albom, author of *Tuesdays with Morrie*

"A courageous story. And the Schefters tell it magnificently. Highly recommended for all collections, this is a captivating account that readers won't be able to put down."
—*Library Journal*

The Man
I Never
Met

A Memoir

Adam Schefter

St. Martin's Griffin
New York

For Joe, who always will be a part of our family.
For Sharri, for whom I've tried to provide all the love and happiness that she once lost.
For Devon, who now has another way to remember his dad.
For Dylan, who brings us all together.
And for all the Maios, who allowed us to honor their son and their family, and who treat me as one of their own.

—

Published in the United States by St. Martin's Griffin,
an imprint of St. Martin's Publishing Group

www.stmartins.com

Designed by Anna Gorovoy

The Library of Congress Cataloging-in-Publication Data
is available upon request.

ISBN 978-1-250-16189-5 (hardcover)
ISBN 978-1-250-21333-4 (signed edition)
ISBN 978-1-250-16190-1 (ebook)
ISBN 978-1-250-23676-0 (trade paperback)

Our books may be purchased in bulk for promotional, educational,
or business use. Please contact your local bookseller or the Macmillan
Corporate and Premium Sales Department at 800-221-7945, extension
5442, or by email at MacmillanSpecialMarkets@macmillan.com.

First St. Martin's Griffin Edition: September 2019

10 9 8 7 6 5 4 3 2 1

1

It is the fall of 2017, and we are getting ready to renovate our house. This is not surprising. We are *always* renovating. My wife, Sharri, can't seem to stop. She loves our house on Long Island, but she is never satisfied with it.

This time, she wants to expand one room, combine two others, enlarge and enclose a patio, and build an attic for storage. I don't entirely understand why we are doing this, but it is what Sharri wants, and I try to do what I can to always make her happy.

Before this renovation, she starts cleaning out her home office. She discovers an old Oxford-brand composition notebook, the kind with the mottled black-and-white cover that you might have used for your spelling or math homework in elementary school.

It is a journal.

Now, I should point out: I have kept my own detailed journal for most of my life. I started doing it when I was in college. My roommates and I were having the greatest time of our lives, but it was all becoming a blur. I struggled to remember the fun we'd had just a week earlier. It bothered me. I decided to keep a log of my actions and thoughts—just a stream-of-consciousness record of my days. On work trips, I keep my journal. On vacation, I keep my journal. It's become as much a part of my day as eating or sleeping; it is something I always get done.

Maintaining a journal has not always been easy, but it is all there for me, every day of my life since 1990, separated into monthly files, every year, on my computer.

Sharri does not keep a journal. She teases me about mine: *Did you remember to write that you went to the bathroom?* But I can go back and find the name of a restaurant where I ate in Los Angeles or my hotel in Philadelphia. I can read about stories I worked on as an NFL reporter—first, covering the Denver Broncos, and then as a league insider for the NFL Network and ESPN. I can learn from my professional and personal experiences.

More importantly, I can go back and remember how I felt at any point in my life. Pride, sadness, frustration, loneliness, joy . . . they're all in there. I can read about where I was, take stock of where I am, and connect the two to measure personal growth.

In her home office, Sharri picks up the journal. What is noteworthy about this journal is that it is not mine.

It is hers.

On the cover, she has written one word: *Devon.*

Inside, there is a single journal entry. It begins:

> *Devon,*
> *This journal for you will never be perfect, the words,*
> *the sentences, may not be proper, but it's important*

you know a little or a lot about your Dad. I'm writing today, Sept. 9, 2002, and as I write I'm watching my peaceful and very beautiful son asleep on my favorite seat outside my swing. You are only 27 months old and who knows when you will read this. Our Dog Riley lays beneath the swing keeping a watchful eye on everything. It is, as I now call them, a "beautiful Sept. 11 morning," no clouds, only sun, just like that day.

I've wanted to do this for a year now, but it was (too) hard. I feel a bit stronger now, a lot older, less tolerant of garbage. Part of me is ecstatic that you are too young to understand what happened to your Dad. The other part is Angry that you never got the chance to know this beautiful, beautiful man who loved you more than his own life!

How horribly unfair this world is. We were all robbed. Your Dad was only 32 years old. He never had a chance to survive those horrible people who did this.

She had stopped writing there.

The story you are reading is not just about September 11. We all know what happened on September 11.

This story is about September 12—and every day after.

It is about finding happiness in the most unlikely places. Sometimes grief leads to love, sadness begets joy, and death makes a family grow larger. The worst days carry us toward some of the best. As much as we'd like to extricate one emotion from the rest, that is impossible.

This is a story about loss and comfort, about pain and beauty.

It is about the steps we take because we want to, and the steps we take because we have no choice.

A lot of families have a story like that.

This is ours.

2

Two months before he died, Joe Maio moved into a new house. He was thirty-two years old, professionally successful, and personally happy, which didn't surprise anybody who knew him. Joe had a gift. He'd had it for so long that he could not remember a time when he didn't have it. The gift was this: He was the rare human being who, from the moment he was born, was completely comfortable in his skin.

It was a gift he could wrap up and hand to others without ever losing it himself. Joe did not care for the social lines that the rest of us draw. Even in his teenage years, when most of us are angst-ridden and unsure of ourselves, he easily mixed friends and family, or popular kids with unpopular ones. He seemed determined to help people overcome the insecurities that he did not have.

The gift gave him a quiet confidence that did not spill into arrogance. Joe expected to do well but not to be handed anything. He did not start fights but occasionally ended them. He sometimes drank alcohol socially but never did it to forget who he was. He liked to kid his friends just enough to let them know he liked them but not so much that it hurt their feelings, and he was wise enough to know the difference. And his gift meant that he could laugh at himself.

Before he moved into his new house, Joe had been living on the Upper West Side of Manhattan with his wife, Sharri, and their one-year-old son, Devon. They liked it there in the city. But Joe and Sharri had sensed it was time to get out, in the way that new parents sometimes get a feeling in their guts that they need a change for the sake of their child. Sharri saw a ten-year-old kid jaywalking on a busy Manhattan street, and she imagined Devon doing that in a few years. She heard city moms talk about fierce competition to get into the best grade schools, and she winced. She didn't want that.

The Maios decided to move to the safety and comfort of the suburbs. They just had to pick a suburb. Joe had grown up in New Jersey, and he wanted to go back. It made sense. His employer, a financial services firm called Cantor Fitzgerald, was planning to move his group out of the highest floors of the North Tower of the World Trade Center to Rumson, New Jersey, in two years.

But Sharri wanted to move closer to where *she* grew up, on Long Island. This made sense, too. She listed all the reasons for Joe. He would be working most of the time anyway. She was a new mother who didn't have any friends in New Jersey. Her family was on Long Island. They could always move to New Jersey if Cantor Fitzgerald followed through on its plans.

Joe thought about it and agreed to move to Long Island. Now they just needed to find a house. They considered building one. New construction would have fit Joe's personality; he liked everything in his life to be clean and just right, from his hair to his clothes to his bedroom. Joe imagined a house with no highway noise, perfectly designed to suit their family. But building a house would take two years, and the Maios didn't want to wait that long.

They found the next-best thing: a house that had just been built. Joe liked that it was new—the floors were unblemished, the toilets not yet used. He was an orderly man, a bit of a germophobe, particular about his possessions. He liked having a house that was completely theirs.

Picture them there, in the summer of 2001: Joe coming home at the end of a long workday, Sharri waiting in the driveway with Devon and their wheaten terrier, Riley. When Joe got home from work, Devon would give his "Da-da" a huge hug. Sometimes Joe would sit Devon on his lap in the front seat of his car and play a song that made him think of Devon. It was called, "With Arms Wide Open," by the band Creed. The band's front man, Scott Stapp, had written the lyrics after he found out he was going to become a father: "With arms wide open/Under the sunlight/Welcome to this place/I'll show you everything."

Joe Maio was a great man. Devon was far too young to understand this, but it was true. Joe was not just great in the way we like to think our parents or spouses are great—*everybody* described Joe that way. He checked all the boxes. Smart. Charming. Good-looking. Athletic. Thoughtful.

And his gift meant that he had a quality that friends had never seen in anybody else: He made people believe that everything would always work out for him. Even more, he made them *happy* that everything would always work out for him.

And he made them think that if they stayed close to him,

everything would work out for them, too. He didn't brag. He didn't act like he was better than other people. He pulled them along for the ride. This only added to their awe of him.

Joe had grown up in a happy family with his brother, Anthony, and their devoted parents, Paula and George. Their house in New Jersey was the house where all the other neighborhood kids wanted to hang out. It had a pool and a finished walkout basement with a wet bar, and everybody was welcome. It didn't matter if Joe's aunts and uncles and cousins were already there. It didn't matter if you were one of the coolest kids in school or if Joe was your only friend. If Joe liked you, you always could come hang out at his house.

Now Joe had a family and his own house. He was ready to build the kind of warm, loving environment that he had enjoyed as a child. His new house on Long Island was much bigger than the Maios' Manhattan apartment, and so parts of it were not furnished yet. Boxes were still unpacked. Pictures had not been hung on the walls. But the Maios were not worried about that. Sharri and Joe Maio had plenty of time.

Three weeks before he died, Joe Maio played golf on a Sunday. This was unusual for him. He absolutely loved golf, but he and Sharri had an agreement: He could play golf on Saturdays, as long as he teed off early and was home in the afternoon, but Sundays were for family time.

Joe worked hard all week. Sunday was their day together. This day was an exception, though. This was for the golf championship at his country club, Tam O'Shanter on Long Island.

Joe's friend Jordan Bergstein had just won the B flight championship at *his* Long Island club, Engineers. The B flight is for lesser golfers—the best of the pretty good—and Joe had ribbed Jordan endlessly for it. *The B championship? Are you sure you want to* tell *people about that?* It was like being the MVP of the junior varsity.

Jordan laughed along with Joe. Teasing was an essential part of their relationship and had been since they met when they were in college—Joe at Boston University, Jordan at American University. They met on spring break. The teasing went both ways, but Jordan knew that Joe had his back. Jordan had a degenerative eye condition, which made it hard for him to follow his golf ball in the air. He never had to ask Joe to do it for him. Joe just did it. Whenever Jordan lost track of the ball, Joe said, "JB, I got you."

And, teasing aside, Jordan knew that Joe Maio never wanted to win the B championship of anything. It was unfathomable to him.

When Joe was a kid, he was such a great skier that other skiers would actually stop on the slopes and watch him. When he was in high school, he had a dream of playing football for Penn State. He was not good enough to play at Penn State, but he believed he was supposed to do things like play football at Penn State. He called their football offices every day until he finally got a coach on the phone, before he ultimately wound up at Boston University. At Cantor Fitzgerald, he became the director of equity derivatives at an unusually young age, a rising star even compared to the firm's other rising stars.

At various stages of Joe's life, he wanted to drive the coolest car, wear the nicest clothes, eat at the best restaurants, date the prettiest girls—and not because he wanted to impress everybody else. He just wanted to experience the best. And when he started to take golf seriously as an adult, he expected to excel at it.

The 2001 Tam O'Shanter Club Championship came down to the final hole. Joe swung a little too hard at his tee shot and did not hit the ball well. His second shot flew over the green. His opponent made par and won.

George hugged his son and congratulated him on going so far. George had followed Joe around the course all day, which had surprised Sharri. To her, golf was one of Joe's hobbies. You don't follow somebody around for hours watching them practice their hobby, even if you love them. But when George watched Joe play golf, he saw something else. He saw Joe as a boy at River Vale Country Club in New Jersey, driving the golf cart before he was legally allowed to drive a car. He saw Joe as a teenager, starting to fall in love with the game. He saw all the weekend days they had spent together on the course, a love of a sport passed from one generation to the next.

Sharri asked George, "Are you really going to follow him around the course all day?"

George said, "One day, when Devon is doing this, you'll follow him."

Two weeks before he died, Joe Maio got into an argument with his wife. It was the kind of argument that could have lingered after Joe died, forever unresolved. He and Sharri had no way of knowing that he was about to die. They did not talk for a day. The silence was torturing both of them.

But while they were not talking, Joe was thinking. He was only thirty-two, and he was still learning what it meant to be married. Joe was used to running the show; he had been doing it, in virtually every social situation, since he was in elementary school. But he was smart enough to know when he was wrong and secure enough to admit it.

Joe found Sharri in the kitchen. Devon was in his high chair. The TV was on. Joe spoke first.

"I love you so much," he told Sharri. "I love our family, and I will do whatever it takes to make this work."

On the day that Joe Maio died, I woke up at 5:00 A.M. Mountain Time in my town house in the Cherry Creek neighborhood of Denver. I was the Denver Broncos' beat writer for *The Denver Post*. I had just gotten back from a weekend in my hometown of New York—visiting family, seeing friends—and then covered a Monday Night Football game in Denver, which happened to be the very first game ever played at the Broncos' new stadium, then called Invesco Field at Mile High.

I was so tired that morning—Tuesday, September 11, 2001— that I didn't even bother showering before heading to a local TV station, KUSA, for a quick on-air segment. I didn't realize it at the time (no one could) but it was one of the very last non-9/11 reports on that TV station, or any TV station in the country, for days.

Moments after my in-studio live shot, at about 6:45 A.M. Mountain Time, I went home. I lived about five minutes from the station. I walked in and went down to my office in the basement. I turned on KBCO radio. Just minutes later, I heard that a plane had hit the North Tower of the World Trade Center.

It did not occur to me that it was a terrorist attack. I just thought, *That's odd*.

I sat in my basement office, listening to news updates on the radio about a crash that seemed like a random accident, and hopefully not terribly tragic. Then another plane hit the South Tower. And at that moment, everyone everywhere knew how serious this was. Only then did I leave my basement office to go upstairs to the living room to turn on my TV. I would sit there for hours on end, transfixed and demoralized. I watched and could not believe what I was seeing. It felt like Pearl Harbor for my generation—only more extreme.

Then a plane hit the Pentagon. And another one crashed in Pennsylvania. It felt like the entire country was under attack. Anything could be attacked next.

I was stunned, overwhelmed, at a complete loss. Weren't we all?

I quickly realized that I knew somebody who worked in the World Trade Center: one of my parents' closest friends, Billy Esposito. I called my parents, Shirley and Jeffrey, to see if they had heard if Billy was safe. They said nobody had heard from him. I was on the phone with my sister, Marni, all day. I didn't know what to do. I had planned to go exercise but didn't. I skipped lunch. I wrote a short story for the newspaper about the NFL possibly canceling that weekend's game.

President George W. Bush had grounded all planes while the country assessed the situation, but that night, as I was in bed, I could hear a plane patrolling the skies overhead. I knew the Air Force Academy was located about sixty miles south of my town house and wondered if what I heard was a simulated flight or another attack. I had no idea what was happening, but I knew this: I actually was scared to leave my own home.

That night, I wrote in my journal:

I don't know that I had ever felt so lonely. Man, did it feel lonely.

It would be days before our country had a firm death toll and years before I heard the name *Joe Maio*. I never met him. I did not know Sharri or Devon.

I did not know that many of Joe's friends thought he was the most impressive person they had ever met. Some of them assumed he would survive the attack on the World Trade Center—not out of hope or denial but because he was *Joe Maio*. To them, he was invincible.

One of Joe's best friends, Adam Gordon, heard the news about the plane hitting the tower and kept working, even as everybody else in the office stopped. Adam had stuff to do. He knew Joe worked at the World Trade Center, but he still was not worried about Joe. Joe would be fine. He always was.

Another friend of Joe's, Casey Cummings, expected to see Joe emerge from the flames of the building, like Superman, carrying another person to safety. It was illogical. Casey knew that. But he still expected it.

Joe's charisma was so powerful and his presence so magnetic that he would hover in his friends' lives long after he had passed. Even now, they talk about him in a way that does not seem real, and they know it. They know they sound like they have polished his image, to make him seem more interesting or more beloved than he actually was, as people often do with the deceased. But they swear this was Joe. This was real. Nothing is exaggerated. Nothing is glossed over.

Jordan Bergstein, who was going through a depressive phase when Joe died, decided immediately that he would live the rest of his life like Joe would have. He still talks about Joe in the present tense. Another friend says Joe's death is what spurred him to reevaluate his on-again, off-again relationship with his girlfriend and get married. Another friend who had fallen out of touch with Joe would say, sixteen years later, that she thought of him almost every day. And another friend says that after Joe died, his mind erased most of his childhood memories that *didn't* include Joe.

So many people would be profoundly changed by Joe Maio's death.

Right near the top of that list, behind Sharri and Devon and Joe's parents and brother, would be me.

Of course, I did not know that as I sat on the couch in my living room in Denver, feeling as alone as I'd ever felt in my life. I just knew I was shocked and devastated—and, as strange as it was, I felt as if there were some sort of force pulling me back to New York.

3

Since this is, at its heart, a September 12 story, let's begin there—on September 12, 2001. My mom had spent the previous night with Billy Esposito's wife, Stevie, at their house. They kept hoping Billy would call or maybe even walk through the front door.

I was in Denver, worrying about Billy and trying to figure out how to live my everyday life. I did a radio show. I went to the gym. I did everything I could to escape but found myself thinking only about Billy. I ate my pineapple and vanilla yogurt for breakfast and read the newspapers. William Safire of *The New York Times* wrote a column headlined NEW DAY OF INFAMY. The news was all so fresh. Even experts were struggling to figure it out. Safire wondered:

Who has been recruiting airline pilots and brainwashing them with dreams of eternal glory?

Two sentences in Safire's column really terrified me:

> The next attack will probably not be by a hijacked jet, for which we will belatedly prepare. More likely it will be a terrorist-purchased nuclear missile or a barrel of deadly germs dumped in a city's reservoir.

Even rereading that now makes me shudder. It was the most powerful and disturbing thing I read that day. I called my mom, and she gave me the news: Nobody from Billy's company, Cantor Fitzgerald, had survived the attack. It was not an official declaration, and some families still were searching and praying for miracles, but they believed that Billy was gone.

It was hard to process that we never would see Billy again. The Saturday night before the attacks, he had gone out to dinner with my parents, and then, three days later, he was gone forever. I spent a lot of time over the next few days thinking about Billy and sobbing.

Memories flooded my brain. I loved talking to Billy, and sports were often a driving force in the conversation. He was a big fan of the Wisconsin Badgers and the New York Mets. My hometown of Bellmore is on the South Shore of Long Island. There are two peninsulas on the south part of the town, and every year on Thanksgiving, we used to play a Turkey Bowl football game at John F. Kennedy High School between families who lived on each peninsula. The Espositos were on one side. We were on the other.

I tried calling Stevie, but she and her daughter, Susie, were in no shape to talk. Billy and Stevie's son, Craig, came to the phone instead. I tried to comfort him, but I was sobbing too hard. *He* ended up having to comfort *me*, which was embarrassing.

I was more than 1,700 miles from New York but felt so close to it. The whole country was in a state of shock. Nobody knew what would be next. Everything seemed to remind everybody of 9/11. One day, I heard air force planes above my apartment building at 4:30 A.M. Another day, I found out that a friend had lost a brother in Vietnam. I'd had no idea. People were sharing experiences they had never shared before. I held a white candle at a vigil and read newspaper stories about those who had died. I wrote in my journal:

Now they're putting names to numbers and you hear these people's death stories and it's real sad.

The week after 9/11, the NFL postponed its games, something it didn't even do in the week when John F. Kennedy was assassinated. The NFL commissioner at the time, Pete Rozelle, always remembered how that was his greatest regret. This time, NFL commissioner Paul Tagliabue did not make the same mistake. The games were, rightfully, postponed.

My first flight after 9/11 was the following week, to Phoenix for a Broncos-Cardinals game. When I got to the airport in Denver to fly out to that game in Arizona, two security guards stopped me, as they did with every car. They heard a hint of my New York accent, and one of them said, "Give New York my love." That stuck with me. But there was a new reality at the airport, with security guards the likes of which we never had seen before. They were checking all people, all bags, making sure nothing got past them. Yet I was disturbed that the

razor blades in my toiletry got through security without anybody stopping me. Like most Americans, I was on edge.

When I got back to Denver after the game, I found the
longest security lines I had ever seen. I had to get in one of
them, because I had another flight. This time, Denver was just
a layover. And a few hours later, I looked out the window and
saw the southwestern tip of Manhattan, across from the Statue
of Liberty. I saw some smoke coming up from where the World
Trade Center used to be. After two of the dreariest weeks in
our country's history, when it felt as if there were a perpetual
sadness that never would lift, I was back in New York for Billy
Esposito's memorial service.

My parents picked me up at LaGuardia Airport. LaGuardia is
usually incredibly busy, but when I walked out of the terminal,
there was an unusually rare sight: Their car was the only one
waiting outside. The only one. It was eerie. The country, especially New York and the surrounding metropolitan area, still
had not come back to life.

The night before the memorial service, we visited the Espositos. We all wanted to help in whatever way we could. My
brother-in-law, Mike Barone, an attorney by trade and a giver
by nature, helped Craig go through Billy's papers. Craig pulled
me aside and told me he had not written anything to say about
his dad at the service. He asked me for advice.

Craig had been a solid student, but he felt like this was the
only time in his life when he *had* to get an A. He thought that
whatever he said at the memorial service would not be good
enough. He asked me for help because I was a writer.

I wasn't sure what wisdom I had for him. I just told him to speak from the heart and to list the attributes about his dad that he admired most. I said that would carry him through, but his question hit me hard. It made me reflect on everything Billy was to his family, my family, and anyone who knew him. On the ride home that night, I broke down again.

The memorial service, at St. Barnabas Church in Bellmore, New York, was excruciating—a stream of people I had known for most of my life, almost all in tears. There was a loose-leaf binder with the names of people from the 9/11 attacks who were missing or dead. It was fourteen pages long.

My mom gave a beautiful eulogy to the more than one thousand people in attendance. Billy was a great family man, a great father, beloved at home and at work. My parents often would travel with Stevie and Billy, taking pictures of the heavyset Billy in unflattering positions. Everyone could laugh at him, but he could laugh at himself. My family had spent many holidays with the Espositos. At those gatherings, conversation almost always reverted back to sports. Billy made me think about sports issues in a different way. He helped fuel my passion. After I was fortunate enough to break into the sports field, he and his family even came to meet me in Washington one year for a Redskins-Broncos game.

Later, Craig Esposito would get a large tattoo on his back. It is a likeness of his father. Above it are two words: *My Hero*.

No one who knew Billy ever could or would forget him. The Espositos' home became a shrine to Billy, with pictures of him everywhere.

I was scared and lonely. I felt a longing for home. My parents were in New York. My sister, Marni, who is three years younger than I am, was there. My brother, Jordan, who is five years younger than I am and has joined me at sporting events since I was in college and he was in high school, lived in an apartment in Long Beach on Long Island.

I wanted to be closer to all of them, but I wasn't really sure what to do about it.

I had a job at *The Denver Post*, covering the Broncos. It's pretty hard to do that from New York. And I didn't want to give up my job. When my parents drove me to the airport that night, with my fears of what was happening in New York and not knowing what was next, I suggested they move to Denver. They declined. They did not want to leave New York. They did not want to leave their family, friends, and life.

I flew back to Denver with a lot on my mind. Billy was only fifty-two when he died. Craig—with whom I remain close to this day—was twenty-five. Billy's daughter, Susie, was twenty-three. Billy didn't get to see their weddings. He didn't get to see his children have children of their own. He missed out on the golden years that were waiting for him as a reward for the life of taking the Long Island Rail Road from Bellmore, New York, to New York City every weekday.

Sometimes I thought about how awful the final minutes of his life must have been, at the top of a burning skyscraper, with smoke rising and no way out. When I would be in a steam room at the gym, and it would get too hot and kind of uncomfortable, I would think about how it wasn't one-millionth of what Billy Esposito experienced when the smoke filled his offices. I thought about him trying to breathe in his final waking moments. That vision haunted me. It still does.

The Esposito and Schefter families had been incredibly close for a long time. We spent Jewish holidays with the Espositos, even though they weren't Jewish. I even babysat for Craig and his sister, Susie, once. I am nine years older than Craig and eleven years older than Susie. It was hard for me to believe they had lost their dad. I tried to imagine their pain, but I struggled to do it.

4

The memorial service for Joe Maio was held at Church of the Presentation in Upper Saddle River, New Jersey. The facts of it were more than the crowd could bear:

Joseph Daniel Maio
Dec. 21, 1968—Sept. 11, 2001

In the days after 9/11, Joe's father, brother, and uncle had gone around New York City, looking for Joe. They were like a lot of families in New York at that time, clinging to hope because hope was all they had. George kept telling himself what he wanted to hear: *Joe is alive . . . he is unconscious . . . he is in a hospital and hasn't been identified yet.* Then, one day, George went to a support meeting for Cantor Fitzgerald families. Somebody said that nobody from Joe's floor had made it down.

The Maios were devastated. No body had been found, but now they knew: Joe was gone.

On September 24, the paid death notice ran in *The New York Times*, a paragraph hopelessly trying to sum up a life:

Beloved husband of Sharri (née Setty). Devoted father of Devon Maio. Loving son of George & Paula Maio. Dear brother of Anthony Maio and his wife Carmela and their three daughters, Nicolette, Dominique, and Julianna . . .

By October 9, Joe was considered legally dead.

As his friends and family gathered for the memorial service, the feelings inside them were too still raw to process, and the world around them was still too chaotic to understand. The nation was still stunned by the attack. War seemed possible. New York felt like a shell of itself. Envelopes containing dangerous anthrax spores were being mailed to media outlets and two U.S. senators; five people would die, and it was unclear who sent the envelopes or who would receive one next.

New York City mayor Rudolph Giuliani had been praised worldwide for going around New York and consoling his city. On September 11, Giuliani had walked two miles north, covered in white ash, for a press conference. He solemnly warned, "The number of casualties will be more than any of us can bear ultimately." It was customary for elected officials to attend the funerals of every police officer or firefighter who died in the line of duty. Giuliani tried, but attending them all was logistically impossible.

"There are too many," he said.

President George W. Bush had announced, in a nationally televised address on September 21, that "our grief has turned to anger, and anger to resolution." This may have been true of the country as a whole, but the people who knew Joe

Maio were still trapped in grief. They had questions they couldn't answer, starting with *Why?*

Just three years earlier, many of the same people had gathered for Joe and Sharri's wedding. It was hard to believe that they were together again for his memorial service, but here they were.

Sharri rode to the memorial service with her parents, Chuck and JoAnn Setty. It was a gray day. Sharri felt sick to her stomach as they drove over the bridges from Long Island. There were constant reminders that Joe's death, as tragic as it was, was part of an even larger tragedy. One of Joe's bosses, Danny LaVecchia, could not even attend the service because so many Cantor Fitzgerald employees had died, and he couldn't attend every service.

At Sharri's request, the Creed song "With Arms Wide Open" was played at the memorial service. Chuck talked about how accomplished Joe was at such a young age and said, "In all the time I knew him, he never once bragged, boasted, or belittled anyone—and he could have easily been tempted to, because he many times found himself in competitive situations." He said two words defined Joe: *quiet dignity.*

Sharri got up to speak. She had written her eulogy in the form of a letter to Joe. It was a perfect mix of humor, honesty, and emotion, and it captured the Joe she loved and the Joe that everybody there knew.

"Let me start off," she said, "with the really important items."

She said: "I have not driven your car, which I know you will be thrilled about, and I have not backed up into a single concrete pole in the last week."

And: "I recently found $1,500 in your car ashtray. The bad news is, Barneys had a year-end shoe sale."

And: "I am sorry to tell you this, but your most treasured possession, your bug vacuum, is broken. I have decided to use your golf clubs in its place."

And: "The dry cleaner has finally figured out how to press your shirts properly, but they still refuse to hand-press your boxer shorts."

There were more than a thousand people there. Every single one of them would have understood if Sharri broke down and couldn't finish, but she got through it. Her sister, Robyn, watched and thought, *I can't believe how composed she is.*

Sharri told Joe that there had been a scorekeeping "mistake" at Tam O'Shanter, and Joe was actually the club champion.

"I would very much appreciate," she said, "if you could come back to pick up your trophy."

From there, she shifted from humorous to heartfelt. She talked about "how sorry I am for not telling you more often how I feel about you." She thanked Joe because he was "always there to listen, and always a very big shoulder to cry on. You achieved more in thirty-two years than most people ever do . . . you will always and forever be my hero."

And she thanked him for "two wonderful things: the chance to have experienced a love that would bind us for life, and our most precious gift: Devon. He is strength, beauty, and kindness. He has a sense of humor that amazes everyone and a presence that takes your breath away.

"I look at him and will forever see you."

The service was like a series of concentric circles with Joe in the middle—everybody tried to console somebody who was in a circle closer to Joe. Acquaintances hugged his good friends, his good friends hugged his closest friends, and his closest friends looked at his family and were overwhelmed.

They had all lost a man they loved, but they lost something else, too: the remaining arcs of their relationships with him.

Sharri missed a chance to raise Devon with Joe and to grow old with him. She read a poem at the service called "Funeral Blues," by W. H. Auden.

Stop all the clocks, cut off the telephone,
Prevent the dog from barking with a juicy bone,
Silence the pianos and with muffled drum
Bring out the coffin, let the mourners come.

Let aeroplanes circle moaning overhead
Scribbling on the sky the message "He is Dead."
Put crepe bows round the white necks of the
public doves,
Let the traffic policemen wear black cotton gloves.

He was my North, my South, my East and West,
My working week and my Sunday rest,
My noon, my midnight, my talk, my song;
I thought that love would last forever: I was wrong.

The stars are not wanted now; put out every one,
Pack up the moon and dismantle the sun,
Pour away the ocean and sweep up the wood;
For nothing now can ever come to any good.

Paula and George missed seeing their son truly grow into being a father. George would always give Joe a kiss on his cheek when he saw him. He had always told Joe, "You don't know what love is until you have your own child."

Joe got to feel that love for less than fifteen months.

And Anthony . . . well, maybe it was most complicated for Anthony. When the boys were little, Anthony was a proud and in some ways protective big brother. Once, when Joe was three or four years old, they went to Disney World in Orlando. Joe saw Mickey Mouse and got excited. Anthony turned to his father and said, "Dad, don't tell Joe, but I know that's not the *real* Mickey Mouse."

They were close, so close—"very, very close," George liked to say. And as close as they were as kids, they were even closer as adults. Their personalities meshed well. As adults, Anthony and Joe spoke every day. They bonded over their shared love of golf. (Both were single-digit handicaps.) Anthony grew up to be a very warm, easygoing guy—the kind of person who shows up at a family function and naturally helps everybody relax and have fun.

They were the best of friends, which made Paula and George beam. Isn't that the dream of every parent who has multiple children? To have children who are happy on their own, but even happier together?

Anthony was the older brother, but when they were adults, Joe was so successful and charismatic that it was hard to imagine him as anybody's younger brother. They were equals. Now, inexplicably and suddenly, Joe was dead. Anthony was devastated. And it felt a little like he had to be Joe's older brother again—protective and strong in a time of need.

Anthony gave a eulogy at the memorial service.

It was the moment that almost everybody there would remember, years later, long after the other details had drifted away.

Along with their three daughters, Anthony and Carmela had also had a son. The son had passed away in utero, devastating Anthony and Carmela. Anthony and Carmela named him Anthony Joseph Maio, after his daddy and his uncle.

Anthony finished his eulogy for Joe by speaking directly to Joe in heaven:

"You watch over my boy up there," Anthony said, "and I'll watch over your boy down here."

That boy down here would forget his daddy. It was inevitable. Everybody at the memorial service knew it. Devon was barely a year old when Joe died, too young to form long-term memories.

When Devon was a toddler, Sharri would sign him up for Mommy and Me classes, and sometimes Devon would go, see another father there, and turn to him and say, "Uppy, uppy, uppy," because he wanted that man to pick him up, like a father would. This is what Sharri had to steel herself against every day—these little bolts of heartbreak hitting her at random times, from all possible directions, for reasons she could not possibly anticipate.

It pained her that Devon did not know Joe. He did not even know what he was missing. As Devon grew up, his father became a name and a face and a series of stories told by other people.

5

After the memorial service, Sharri did not know where to start the rest of her life. The shocking death of a loved one makes you feel that everything has come to a standstill, but of course, it hasn't. Life keeps moving around you. The little boy who raced to hug his father on weekday evenings was still there, in the house, far too young to understand that his father was not coming back. Sharri had to raise a child whose life had just begun while she mourned a husband whose life had just ended.

Her existence had a past and a future, and somewhere in there, she had to find the present.

She was terrified that something would happen to Devon, but she was also terrified that something would happen to *her*, leaving Devon an orphan. There were reports and rumors that terrorists might target major bridges. Sharri was scared of driving on them. She didn't want to get trapped. Even when she visited the Maios in New Jersey, George was so generous and kind that he would come pick her up on Long Island and drive her back to New Jersey so she didn't have to be at the wheel.

Flying was out of the question. Sharri was sure she would never get on an airplane again.

There were many days when she didn't know how she would go on. She did not want to leave the house, but she also did not want to be in it. She did not have that many memories of Joe there—they had only lived in the house for two months. They had not finished unpacking. She was still decorating.

But the house was a physical reminder of the life they'd planned to live.

Being there made her uncomfortable, lonely, and depressed. She would wake up in the morning and desperately want to get out of the house. Then she would be out in public and want to go back inside.

She never turned the television off in her house. Ever. It was on twenty-four hours a day, even when she slept, and never tuned to the news—it was cartoons, or reruns of *Seinfeld* and *Friends*, or whatever came on after the reruns of *Seinfeld* and *Friends*. The programming was not the point. The TV was her antidote for the quiet, her weapon against the void.

She would ask herself, *How the hell did I wind up here? How does this happen? Why Joe?* She did not think she would make it through that first year. She didn't see how she could.

She had survivor's guilt. She thought, *Why did this happen to him? Why not me?* There was no answer. There is no logical reason why Joe Maio died at age thirty-two—or at least, no reason that makes sense. He was in the wrong place at the wrong time.

She went through their photo albums. She watched their wedding video. But everything was colored by his death now.

She remembered their honeymoon in Italy, when they kept hearing Andrea Bocelli's hit song "Time to Say Goodbye," and what had been a fond memory was just sad now. Even that Creed song that had meant so much to Joe, "With Arms Wide Open," brought more heartache: "If I had just one wish/Only one demand/ I hope he's not like me."

In the summer of 2001, she had hired a painter to paint a mural inside their house, an outdoor scene inside the house full of flowers and grass and blue skies. The original plan was to paint it gray, but Sharri had added color. She wanted it to be full of life.

The painter was in the house, working on the mural, when the planes hit the towers.

After Joe died, Sharri decided she wanted to move out, to a condominium on Long Island—something smaller and more manageable and with fewer reminders of what had just happened. But the real-estate market had cratered. She didn't get any offers on the house. She pulled it off the market.

The painter kept coming back. Sharri wanted something beautiful to emerge from this ugly, horrific time. The painter had said he would need a month to finish the mural. He took six. She did not fire him.

Paula and George Maio did not know where to go or what to do. They had had such a good life until tragedy struck. They were practically kids when they got married; George was twenty-one, and Paula was nineteen. They had met at a bowling alley, where she asked him to drive her home. For more than three decades, they had built their lives around the two boys, Joe and Anthony, and now one of them was gone.

A few weeks later, George went back to Tam O'Shanter Country Club, Joe's old club. Not much time had passed since George had walked the course to watch Joe finish second in the club championship—proud of his boy and the success he had become, excited about the life in front of him.

This time, George was there to clean out his son's locker. He found a brand-new putter, wrapped in cellophane, with the price tag on it.

The Maios were literally picking up the pieces of Joe's life.

Paula and George were in extreme emotional pain. Losing Joe was the biggest reason, of course, but it wasn't the only one. There was the complete shock of it. There was the lingering uncertainty—at first, they hoped he was alive, then they had to accept that he wasn't, but they still didn't know exactly how he died. Had he stayed in the World Trade Center or jumped when the heat and smoke became overwhelming?

And then there was the fact that somebody had *chosen* to do this to Joe—it wasn't a disease or a random act of nature. That is difficult to reconcile: how other humans could choose to destroy the people who mean the most to you. The Maios are also warm, empathetic people, and they were keenly aware that their tragedy was just one of many. A lot of Joe's friends and coworkers at Cantor Fitzgerald had also perished in the attacks. George felt like the world was coming to an end.

The Maios took their love for Joe and directed it toward Devon. He was just a toddler who needed attention and love like any other child, and with Joe gone, Devon would become the glue that connected Paula and George to Sharri as they grieved.

Devon and Sharri spent every Christmas Day at the Maios'

house in New Jersey. And Paula and George would frequently drive to Long Island to spend some time with Devon. George would sleep at Sharri's house two nights a week. George taught his grandson the words to "What a Wonderful World," a song written by Bob Thiele and George David Weiss and made famous by Louis Armstrong.

They would sing, together:

I see trees of green, red roses too
I see them bloom for me and you

Devon alone made them all believe it could be a wonderful world again. He saved lives without knowing it; he made days without realizing it. He gave the whole family strength. When you are in the depths of grief, especially after a loved one dies so young, you need to know that the days ahead will be brighter. That was what Devon did for Sharri, Paula, George, and even George's mom. They would hold him or play with him or sing to him, and that alone would give them the energy to keep going. Devon gave them what they needed more than anything else: He gave them tomorrow.

In the next circle was Anthony. Not too long after 9/11, Anthony took a job on a desk at Cantor Fitzgerald. He was bright and capable, but the move still surprised a lot of people who knew him. He had been a civil engineer, not a trader. He had a master's degree in construction management, not business administration.

And he just never seemed like the Cantor Fitzgerald type. Anthony was your buddy down the street, not your man in the refined world of international finance. It was hard to know if he was looking for a career or his brother.

And in the next circle was a man they called Little Joe Maio. He was Joe's cousin, three years younger—when Little Joe was born, everybody called him Baby Joe, until he was well past babyhood and Paula, his aunt, said, "You've got to stop calling him that." That's when he became Little Joe, and the name stuck.

Joe and Little Joe were closer than many brothers. It was a different relationship from what Joe had with Anthony, because Joe got to be the bigger brother from the start, and the role suited him. They had sleepovers. They entered roller-skating contests together. Little Joe went to a lot of Joe's baseball games.

Joe would take Little Joe skiing on the toughest hills. Joe would look down at the mountain, survey the moguls, get a path in mind, and take off, weaving and doing jumps and daffies all the way down. Little Joe was not as skilled—he went side to side slowly down the mountain. Joe always waited for him at the bottom so they could back go up the mountain on the chairlift together.

Little Joe followed Joe to Boston University, where they lived together. Little Joe always looked up to his cousin, even as an adult. When Little Joe started working at Saks Fifth Avenue, Joe would visit. And when Joe would leave, men and women would ask Little Joe, *Who was that?*

When the planes hit the towers, Little Joe was living on Nineteenth Street, in Chelsea. He stayed put initially. He thought Joe would come to his apartment, since it was walking distance from the World Trade Center and Joe knew where it was. He stayed there into the night, hoping his cousin would come to his door. Then a friend came by, and they went to hospitals. They put his name on every list, hoping somebody would see Joe and call.

Many years later, when Joe was long gone and Little Joe was in his forties, he would think about his cousin. He would go trick-or-treating with Devon and color Easter eggs with him.

Little Joe thought about the polish that we so often apply to the dead—the things that we say because they are nice, even if they aren't completely honest. He was sure this was different. With Joe, all the compliments rang true. Little Joe was reminded of Joe in ways big and small, and whenever a family member talked to him. Long after Joe was gone, his cousin was still proud to be known to all as Little Joe.

The friends were in the next, larger concentric circle, further from Joe than family. Many of them were devastated and bewildered. They needed to sort out their feelings of love and grief, but that would take time. They had similar emotions and thoughts, even if they didn't share them with each other. Nobody attacked life like Joe Maio. The idea that he was suddenly gone was hard for his friends to process.

The combination of Joe's age (thirty-two) and the time in history (2001) meant that many of his friends were only in sporadic touch with Joe at that point. There was no Facebook. Email was something you checked when you turned on your computer, not your phone. Keeping in touch took more work than it does now. Joe's friends were in their early thirties, just starting to settle down, living hectic lives with burgeoning careers and new families that left them too busy to reminisce about the high school or college years. They felt no urgency to reconnect. They had all the time in the world, until they didn't.

His friends took their memories of Joe, and they scattered like autumn leaves—a cluster here, a lonely one over there.

Friends who had been so important to Joe when he was fifteen had moved to the periphery when he was twenty-one. People he didn't meet until he was in his midtwenties had become some of his closest friends.

Joe may not have realized this, but it was true: Even the people who did not keep in touch with him thought about him all the time.

His charisma was such that it is common for childhood friends to remember the precise moment they'd met him. Cory Tovin met him at their town's pool, on the grass next to the beach volleyball court. Lori Sloves first saw him pushing an audiovisual cart through a hallway in first grade. Jeff Heitzner met him when he was invited to Joe's house by their mutual friend, Scott Benincasa. Duane Tarrant was in summer camp in 1979; friends asked Duane, who is African American, and Joe to reenact the Rocky Balboa–Apollo Creed fight from that summer's hit, *Rocky II*. The end of their relationships with Joe had come suddenly, but the beginnings remained etched in their minds.

They all had their Joe Maio stories. The stories don't really have a theme or a pattern, except that people remember them so well and say they could only have happened to Joe Maio. When they told people they lost a friend on 9/11, they tried to explain that he was unlike anybody they'd ever met. They thought of him as a superhero in small ways.

Heitzner tells this story: One day, when Joe and Jeff were at a bar in New York City with some female friends, a stranger started giving them a hard time. Joe didn't take that from anybody. He responded verbally. He and his friends were asked to leave the bar. They did, and when they got outside, four guys came running after Joe and Jeff.

Jeff took his sport jacket off and threw it on the sidewalk. He was ready for a fight. He didn't need to be ready.

The four guys came running at Joe, and he took them out, one by one—*pop-pop-pop*—until the fourth guy got smart and ran away before Joe could hit him. Jeff remembers driving home that night, thinking about those four guys and how they must have been asking themselves, *How did we just get our asses kicked by one guy?*

Joe just did stuff like that. You couldn't explain it. And maybe the telling part is not that he took the guys out but that he was so willing to *try* to take all four guys out.

This was not a totally isolated incident, either. When Joe worked at Boston University, he worked as a bouncer at a club called Paradise. One day, he was working and he saw a fight across the street, and in the middle of the fight was Cory Tovin. Joe ran across the street, threw off his jacket, and took on the guy who was fighting Cory. He was fearless, and he did not take crap from anybody.

One day, before he was a teenager, Joe and his friend Duane Tarrant were riding home on a bus from a camp trip, and they had to pee. They asked the counselor to pull over. The counselor said no. They thought he was being a jerk, and they really had to go. They found a bag to pee in. The counselor found out about it and started screaming at them.

Duane was terrified that word would get back to his parents.

He would get kicked out of camp. He was *in trouble*, as kids say—every child's fear. He started crying.

Joe was having none of it.

"Duane, what are you getting upset about?" Joe said. "We had to go to the bathroom, and he wouldn't pull over. Are they going to kick us out of camp because we had to go to the bathroom? I will get home and tell my parents *exactly* what happened."

It was both totally logical and an amazing thing for a pre-teen to say. How do you describe that attitude? It's not really courage. Joe just had a comfort with himself, and a confidence that he was doing the right thing and everything would work out, no matter what anybody else said. You don't see that from too many ten- or eleven-year-old kids. You don't even see that kind of confidence from that many adults—real, authentic confidence, not false bravado. It even helped some of his friends develop confidence in themselves.

Now Joe was gone, but his friends were all still alive, still moving, still connecting and disconnecting and reconnecting with people. Many of them were not sure if they should try to keep Joe's memory alive and talk to his family, or if they should stay in the background and leave his family alone. It was hard to know what to say. Where was the space between too close and too far?

Jeff Heitzner made a decision: He would leave Sharri, Paula, and George alone. He had known them since he was a kid, but he decided he would not keep in touch, because he did not want to remind them of Joe. Finally, after a few years, another friend set him straight: *Everything* reminded them of Joe. He could not remind them of Joe's death any more than he could remind them they had skin or that they spoke English. Joe's death was a constant part of their lives.

Jeff realized his friend was right. He sent George an email, and George was grateful that one of Joe's old buddies had been thinking of him. They kept in touch after that.

And then there was the one friend who was in such shock that he didn't think about moving on, because he still didn't believe Joe was dead. His name was Adam Gordon. His denial was so overwhelming that he had gone to Joe's memorial service fully expecting Joe to walk in.

Adam Gordon was in eighth-grade math class when he met Joe Maio, and Adam would remember it as one of the seminal moments of his existence, so important that if you ask Adam what his life would have been like if he *hadn't* met Joe, he says, "It's inconceivable."

From the start, their relationship was defined by two facts: Joe liked Adam. But Adam *needed* Joe. Adam came from a dysfunctional family, and he spent the early years of his life feeling unloved. He was too chatty for his own good, and the more masculine boys in school bullied him. Adam did not have many friends. Joe decided he would be one for him.

They were an unlikely pair, something out of a sitcom or a movie that nobody would believe. Joey was the star that everybody loved. Adam was the wisecracking sidekick that nobody understood. Joe's other pals were taken aback by their friendship; at best, they didn't understand, and at worst, they resented it.

Joe didn't care. He liked Adam. Joe didn't need anybody

else's approval. He welcomed everybody. There were no airs, no obvious teenage insecurities, no desperation to fit in, no impulse to prove he was more important than other people, no worries about his image. He did what he wanted. He did not judge.

When Joe became a teenager, girls started to fall for him, and he knew it and enjoyed it, but he didn't flaunt it. He just lived. He had an air of confidence about him that was unlike most people. He saw the world differently. He seemed devoid of angst.

He would tell his buddies to come over to his house and sit by the pool and have a burger off the grill, and they would get there and see his uncles and cousins were there, and they would wonder if they were intruding on a family event. They would say, "Are you sure, Joey? Are you sure it's OK for us to be here?" He always said yes. Of course they were welcome. Why would it be any different with Adam Gordon?

Some of his friends had a reason it was different with Adam: They thought Adam was in love with Joe. It was easy to understand why. Joe was this good-looking, popular guy. Adam was this boy who would drop everything to be around Joe, and Adam seemed gay. Adam never said if he was gay, but many of his classmates assumed he was because of his voice and how he acted. He just seemed so obviously gay to them.

It did not help that sometimes Adam would try on the girls' clothes.

One day, in high school, Adam Gordon was walking down the hallway when somebody called him a *fag*. This was not surprising. It was the early 1980s. The word was commonly applied to boys like Adam.

The surprise was what came next: Two football players

whom Adam had never met stood between him and his tormentor.

"He's our boy," one of them said. "And he's our boy because he is Joey's boy."

Adam was a fearful child. Joe pushed Adam to take risks. Sometimes they would drive Anthony's car around town before they had licenses. Joe loved skiing, and Adam had never done it, so one day Joe took Adam to Hunter Mountain, a ski resort in New York, and up a chairlift to the top of Hellgate, a black-diamond trail, and said, "Off you go!" Joe pushed Adam down the hill. The ski patrol had to get Adam, but he had confronted another fear.

They stuck together the way only childhood friends can really stick together. The two of them would make cinnamon rolls after school. Adam blew off most of a summer camp so he could spend his days with Joey. When Adam's mother screamed at him, Joe mediated.

One day in the 1980s, Joe Maio and Adam Gordon sat in Joe's bedroom, surrounded by gray Formica furniture.

Joe asked Adam a question.

"Do you think you're gay?"

Adam did not think he was gay. Adam didn't really understand what *gay* meant. He had seen gay people in movies, but they were all caricatures. He didn't feel like one of them. So, no, he did not *think* he was gay. He assumed he was heterosexual, like everybody else.

Joe said, "I love you no matter what."

Most childhood relationships fade. This one did not. Joe and Adam lived together on the Upper East Side of Manhattan when they were in their twenties. Joe gave Adam his leftover clothes; most of them didn't fit Adam, but he kept some of them, like Joe's Giorgio Armani ties. They were so close that they would hold conversations through a closed bathroom door when one of them had to use the toilet.

Sometimes they would go to clubs together, and they would each come home with a woman. Then, the next morning, Joe and Adam would go to brunch, and Adam would wonder why other people seemed to enjoy sex so much. What was so great about it? He was baffled.

Joe's favorite restaurant at that time was Il Mulino, a fine Italian restaurant in Greenwich Village. He liked when Adam went with him, but Adam was making $24,000 a year working in retail; Il Mulino was out of his price range. Joe always told Adam, "Whatever you normally pay for dinner, you pay. I'll pay the rest."

Eventually, Joe married Sharri, and Adam married one of Sharri's best friends . . . but still, the bond between them meant everything to Adam. Joe understood him in a way that almost nobody else did. One year, Joe sent a Häagen-Dazs ice cream birthday cake to Adam's office. Adam was overwhelmed with gratitude. It was not just a cake to him. It was Joe's way of acknowledging that Adam's family had never really celebrated his birthday, and so Joe would.

Adam had relied on Joe so heavily for so long that his death felt like somebody had removed the spine of his own existence, leaving him no choice but to collapse. Life without Joe? *Inconceivable.*

For years afterward, people knew not to mention Joe Maio's death to Adam Gordon. He couldn't discuss it with anybody. He could barely accept that it had happened. He would dream that Joe found him. He would walk down Manhattan streets and be so convinced that he saw Joe's face in a crowd that he would lose his breath.

Joe's death shook Adam so hard that Adam quickly forgot many of the other names and faces from his childhood. People stopped Adam on the street because they remembered him well from when they grew up, and he had no idea who they were. Many of his childhood memories disappeared in the smoke that lingered after 9/11. All that remained was Joe.

The largest circle surrounding Joe's death included the entire country. Joe did not just die young and tragically. He died young and tragically on 9/11. This made him part of our national story, and Sharri had to reconcile the fact that her personal tragedy was also America's. There were thousands of stories, thousands of TV hours, and hundreds of books dedicated to the attack that took her husband's life. She felt this weird sensation of being alone while everybody was watching.

Sharri had to cling to the spirit and memory of Joe as he really was, instead of just a small character in a larger story or a name in an article. One of the newspaper stories about Joe did not sit right with her. She did not think it adequately captured him. She felt like the times she tried to honor his memory, the words did not do him justice.

The tributes were well meaning but still inadequate. How can you sum up a person's life in a few paragraphs, as *The New York Times* attempted to do with its Portraits of Grief thumbnail sketches on each of the 9/11 victims?

You could tell Joe Maio stories all day and night. You could say that when he was in tenth grade, he charmed his biology teacher by crooning an old Paul Anka tune: "Put your head on my shoulder, hold me in your arms." Or that when he was in college, he and his roommate Cory Tovin would stand in their separate showers in the dormitory and sing an old Mamas and Papas song: "California dreamin' . . . on such a winter's day . . ."

Or you could tell people about the night when he was a kid and he and his friends decided to go around town, knocking on house doors and running down to the bottom of the drive-way. When somebody answered the door, they would stand there and start singing "Happy Trails." Most people would just look out at them and shake their heads. *What are you guys doing?* They thought it was hilarious. They were kids and it was summertime, and Joe seemed to know how to have fun and stake his independence without doing anything dangerous. He knew where that line was.

You could say he held a pool party when his parents were out of town and collected a cover charge at the door as an example of his daring. You could say he took black football team-mates into Little Italy in Manhattan for the Feast of San Gennaro to show how he embraced everybody.

You could say he liked to have a good time by filling bath-tubs with bottles of beer on the Jersey Shore, or you could say that his idea of a good time was not always the same as every-body else's. Joe drank but did not smoke—not cigarettes and not pot. When he was in college, he went to Jamaica for spring break with almost all his Zeta Beta Tau fraternity. When a man goes to spring break in Jamaica with a bunch of fraternity brothers and does not smoke pot, he needs something to do. He and Cory Tovin gave a few Jamaican kids twenty bucks to give them a tour of the countryside, with its ganja and sugar-cane fields, while their friends stayed back and got high.

If you wanted to give people a sense of his compassion, you could talk about the time when his puppy had a cold and Joe slept with him on the kitchen floor in his pajamas, or you could say that when his mother had an aneurysm in 1991, he wrote a beautiful note to her, not knowing if she would survive.

You could say he had a love of adventure but a firm belief in doing what he felt was right. As a little boy with his parents at a Chevrolet dealership, he took caps off tires and brought them home. Then he felt guilty and told his mom. She took him back to the dealership to apologize. By the end of the apology, the dealer was giving him candy.

You could talk about his ability to get you to do what he wanted—and make you think it was what you wanted. It was almost funny, the way he pulled it off. This was how he managed to get his close friend Jordan Bergstein to sign off on his close friend Adam Gordon living with them, even though Jordan and Adam had never met and didn't really have much in common.

He said to Jordan, "You know, JB, I was thinking . . ."

Jordan: "Yeah?"

Joe: "Ah, forget it."

Jordan: "What?"

Joe: "Never mind."

Jordan: "Come on, tell me."

Joe: "OK. I have this friend Adam . . ."

But what does that story say to you? Does it sound charming or conniving? If you hear that Joe once went inside a packed bar "just to say hi" to some people, then stayed and drank beer while two friends were stuck outside in pouring rain, and then defended himself to those two friends by saying, "Hey, am I supposed to know the weather took a change?" . . . well, what would you think? He might sound like a jerk unless you heard his friends tell the story, laughing so hard at the memory. They knew Joe far too well to think he was a jerk; that, in fact, is why they love the story so much. Only somebody as caring and pure-hearted as Joe could get away with that.

Friends always talk about how women loved him, but the stories make him sound like a player. He wasn't, really. At any given moment in his life, he was just as likely to be in a serious relationship as playing the field. When he was in high school, he and his friend Lori Sloves would lie in his waterbed together . . . and read *The Great Gatsby* aloud to each other. Does that sound like a player to you?

The allure of Joe was not in a story. It was in how he carried himself and in the feeling he gave people. He made them feel good about themselves. Sharri missed that feeling so much that she wasn't sure how she would survive.

They had met in a summer rental house in the Hamptons in the early 1990s. Sharri was staying there. Joe showed up one night with a friend and crashed at the house. She found him lying on the couch downstairs and thought, *Who the hell is* this *guy?*

She went outside to lie by the pool. He went outside to hit on her. She was not impressed. That day, he said something that bothered her. She responded with, "It was really nice meeting you," and walked away. She did not expect to see him again, but Joe Maio was never good at accepting rejection; it happened so rarely that it seemed like it must be a mistake.

He knew the manager of the rental house, and he got the guy to track down Sharri. He called her and convinced her to go on a date in the city. Il Mulino. Of course. They dated for four years, off and on—two pieces that were undeniably attracted to each other but did not always fit together snugly.

Joe was self-assured and had been raised in a home where his mother and father had traditional gender roles. Sharri was headstrong and didn't take any crap from anybody. They each had to adjust. Joe was not a morning person, to put it mildly, and one day he woke up and started yelling at Sharri. She kicked him out of her apartment and told him never to come back. He left, but he called her a day later. He listened and he learned, and he became the man that Sharri wanted to live with forever.

Joe was ambitious, but he was also tender. Sharri liked the combination. You could throw yourself at Joe Maio and not regret it.

He liked the finer things in life, and the finer things seemed like they were meant for him. He would spend $2,500 on a custom-made suit and wear it comfortably. He didn't seem like he was compensating for something. Joe reminded Sharri of Hubbell Gardiner, the carefree Robert Redford character in *The Way We Were*. He had the effortless cool of a movie star.

6

Spring 2006: I sat in the back seat of Craig Esposito's car with tears in my eyes. Craig's girlfriend, Heather, whom he would marry, sat in the front passenger seat. They knew why I was on the verge of crying.

I was lost.

Thirty-nine years old, single, childless, and lost.

Craig and Heather tried to comfort me.

"Adam, you'll meet somebody . . ."

"Obsessing won't do anything for you . . ."

"You have to let this go . . .

I pretended to listen, but they knew I was only really pretending. Craig felt like I was agreeing with them just because I was supposed to. I was in such a bad place that I could think of nothing else—so upset I could only think of being upset. I was putting a lot of pressure on myself.

It must have been a little sad for Craig to see me that way. When he was seven, he decorated his room with sports posters and team pennants to copy my bedroom; mine had a circle of sports teams' pennants for as long as I could remember—the Knicks and Lakers and Celtics, which I still can envision in my mind today. When he was fifteen, he told people that he was proud to know a professional sportswriter. We were long past the point where he looked up to me. But here I was, pushing forty and falling apart.

How did I get there? Let's start by going back a few years. I had been married once before, in the 1990s. I met a woman at a party on Christmas Eve, and our relationship unfolded in three acts: We dated for fifteen months, we were engaged for fifteen months, and we were married for fifteen months.

My first wife was a really nice, sweet, smart, successful woman who was finishing law school when we met. She checked all the boxes. I liked her. I was new to Colorado, but she was from there, so her family became my family. A lot of my friends were getting married, and I didn't want to lose her. I also wasn't sure I wanted to marry her, either, but getting married seemed to be the next logical step in life. One day, my mother said, "What's the difference? You already act like an old married man anyway." And I thought, *She's right. I might as well try this.*

But in those forty-five months, I never really felt totally comfortable in the relationship. My friends could all see it. They didn't tell me this at the time, but they were taking bets at my wedding on how long it would last, establishing the over/under. When I finally ended the marriage, I felt awful about the whole thing. We were in a relationship that had run its course, which happens—but there never should have been a wedding in the middle of it. I never should have gotten married in the first place. I wasn't ready for it. It was an unfair thing to do to a good woman.

I told her she would realize someday that ending the marriage was best for both of us. I said, "Listen, one day you're going to thank me for this."

And sure enough, a few years later, we happened to speak on the telephone, and she said, "You were right. You said it would be the best thing that happened to me, and you were right." She had gotten married, started a family, had children of her own, and gone on from her job as a public defender to become a judge. I was happy for her and relieved for both of us. It brought closure to the whole issue.

The truth was that, at that time, I loved my career more than I loved anything. I have always been extremely driven. It's borne, I believe, out of my fear of failure. The idea of failing, missing on something, is a concept I can't stomach. When I was a kid, I never missed a day of school. I mean *never*. I had a perfect attendance record. I took pride in that.

When I became an NFL reporter, I didn't have a lot of obvious writing talent, but I wanted to try to be the best reporter I could. It didn't matter how many hours I had to work or what holidays I would have to skip to report. I was willing to do whatever it took. I knew that family life complements work life for some people, and they find balance, but that was not me when I was in my twenties. My job was everything; I spent my mornings, afternoons, nights, weekends with it. I was married to it.

Covering an NFL team for a newspaper feels glamorous at times, but at its essence, it is really a blue-collar job. You scramble, make phone calls, transcribe interviews, type your stories, file them, do your best not to get beat on a story—and then do it all again the next day and every day. I loved it. The grind wears some people down, but it energized me. I lived, breathed, ate, and drank it. People would ask how long I could keep going at that pace. I honestly thought I could—and might— spend the rest of my life covering the Denver Broncos. It would have been an honor.

For years, I had a life in Denver that was unconventional but fulfilling, at least for a while. I spent my summers at the Broncos' training camp on the University of Northern Colorado campus, in Greeley, Colorado, about seventy-five miles northeast of Denver. I spent my fall weekends with the Broncos. I spent Thanksgiving, Christmas, New Year's Eve, New Year's Day at practice, or in the Broncos' press room, or on the road covering them. For fifteen years, I had covered the Broncos, writing two or three stories per day throughout the year, feeding a fan base that was insatiable.

Football players spend an incredible amount of time at their team's facility, and coaches and executives famously work from before dawn to after dusk. I was a single guy. I had nowhere else to go, nothing else I really wanted to do. Their schedule fit mine. I developed close relationships with a lot of them. Eventually I helped Mike Shanahan, Terrell Davis, and Bill Romanowski write books. Football people became the people I saw most often. They became part of the landscape of my life.

But still, they weren't family. And as I grew older, that life started to feel emptier to me. Players came and went. So did coaches. I still loved being around them, and I still loved covering the NFL, but I also wanted something more.

After I got divorced, my parents would say that I would settle down when I found a woman I wanted to spend time with as much as I wanted to work. I felt like I was at that point, or certainly getting close to it. I just needed to meet the perfect woman.

And when I say perfect, I mean *perfect*. I wanted to fall in love so badly that I'd built up this romantic ideal in my head. I wanted a flawless person, a spotless résumé, everything to be *exactly* right.

I remember one night when I was with my uncle Marty Freedman in Denver. He wasn't actually my uncle, but I thought of him that way. When I moved to Denver, he was the only person in the state that I had any previous connection to; he was my aunt's uncle, and he looked after me as if I were his nephew. On my very first Sunday in Denver, he had me over to his house to watch the Broncos play in Los Angeles against the Raiders. The first Broncos game I watched in Denver was with him, which was appropriate.

Marty was a huge sports fan, and he would take me to Nuggets or Avalanche games whenever one of his children, or grandchildren, didn't want to go. Sometimes I was his backup plan, but I never minded being his backup plan.

He did so much more for and with me, taking me to meals and games, offering me advice, becoming someone I loved very much. We went to regular breakfasts in Cherry Creek, discussed dating and finances, and when something good happened to me, he was as proud of me as one of my parents would be.

Years later, after our relationship strengthened, we went to a Denver Nuggets game, and he said, "You know now, at this stage of your life, when you do get married, you're going to be marrying someone with kids or someone divorced?"

I was almost offended by it. This was both silly and hypocritical—after all, I had been divorced myself. But I was oblivious to that. He was being practical and real, but I wasn't interested in practical and real. I was locked in on what I perceived to be the perfect romantic story. And when I didn't find it after years of looking in Denver, I decided I needed to make a change.

I loved Denver. I still do. Even now, the city runs through my soul, but after seventeen years there, the city felt socially suffocating—I'd run into the same people everywhere I went, and every woman I dated seemed to know the same people I knew. I don't know if I was depressed at the time, but for as well as I knew Denver, I felt lost. Most of my peers were married. Many of them had kids. It felt like life was leaving me behind.

I had the freedom to move because I had switched jobs. In early 2004, while I was working for *The Post*, I got a call from somebody at the fledgling NFL Network. His name was Eric Weinberger, and he was interested in hiring me. I talked to Eric and the people he worked with there for six months before they offered me a job. They never said what they might want me to do. It was this nebulous interest. League-owned TV networks were a relatively new phenomenon; MLB Network would not be launched until 2009. Nobody knew if this would work or what it would be like. But finally, Weinberger called me back and said, "All right, this is what we want you to do: parting shots like Mike Lupica and information like Peter King."

To my ears, those were magical words—a winning combination. *Sports Illustrated*'s Peter King was—and is—one of the best-known and best-read NFL reporters in the country. He was also a mentor and a friend. Lupica had been the best-known sports columnist in New York since I was a kid, and his "Parting Shots" on *Sports Reporters* was an ESPN staple. It made me seriously consider leaving something I had poured the first fifteen-plus years of my career into doing.

I agonized over it for days. Do you make the jump and leave the newspaper field in which you've honed your skills since college? Or stay on the path that you've been on, that you love, that you dreamed about since working for the student newspaper, *The Michigan Daily*, at the University of Michigan? Newspapers were still considered safe harbors for a journalist. Back then, newspaper reporters looked at TV reporters with some mild disdain. I had some trusted friends and advisors who urged me not to make the mistake of a lifetime, not to leave the career that I was building in newspapers, not for a league-owned network. I still can hear their voices today. "Don't do it, don't do it . . ."

But the more I thought about the NFL Network job, the more I liked the idea of it. Then, one Thursday in July 2004, I was a panelist on ESPN's *Sports Reporters*, shooting the show at the then ESPN restaurant in Times Square, in the center of New York City. Mike Lupica was one of the panelists that day. He forgot his sport coat and had to go to the nearby Macy's to buy a replacement one before the show. After the show, as I was leaving the studio and my father was driving me back to LaGuardia Airport to fly back to Denver, the NFL Network finally called with a firm offer.

It was for more than twice what I was making at *The Post*.

And I knew in my gut that my time at the newspaper, and maybe in newspapers, was done.

My next thought was: *When do I start?*

Getting that offer while my father was driving me to the airport was one of those life-changing moments that always will stay with me. It is still one of the most memorable and most exciting moments of my career. Sharing it with my father, a huge sports fan on his own, meant so much. My father usually is reserved and soft-spoken, but even he got excited at the idea of me now making the switch.

I still can picture right where we were, pulling up to LaGuardia Airport, when the offer came in. I went inside, checked in for my flight, and began calling people from a pay phone right in front of the gate—this was in the days before everybody had a cell phone—to let them know I would be leaving newspapers to try out television. At the time, it was considered a bold move, leaving newspapers for television, and especially a league-owned network, but I was ready to take the leap. With the network being based in Los Angeles and the league offices in New York, I could have gone home then if I chose. But at the time, I was dating a woman from Colorado, so moving was not at the forefront of my thinking. Yet after we broke up the next year, I started to feel that pull again. I felt like New York City was calling me home.

When I left *The Denver Post* for the NFL Network, my work had morphed from the daily grind and rush of a pro football beat to something even more intense. I was just getting my feet into the national reporting world and trying to acclimate to that. It was a big adjustment, print to TV, covering one team compared to thirty-two, and these professional changes had an impact on my personal life. My job was my first love, but I was trying to find another love to complement it.

The new job provided me with the ability to pick a new city to live, any city I wanted. There was something about New York that was especially alluring. I never had the opportunity as a professional to work in New York. My family still was living there—my parents in Bellmore, my sister and brother-in-law and their children in Melville, and my brother in Long Beach.

And so I acted on the urge that I'd first felt when I saw those hijacked planes hit the tallest buildings in New York City: I moved home.

In December 2005, I found an apartment on the Upper West Side of Manhattan. I fell in love with the apartment immediately. I wrote in my journal:

> *I can't tell you how psyched I was . . . Felt like I had started a whole new chapter in my life, and this was very therapeutic. Just left me with a great feeling, one day after feeling terribly uneasy about everything and wondering if I could make the move. But I went bold and did it and was happier than I thought I would be. Was really happy.*

I planned to move in when the football season ended. I had high hopes for my new life. I was living closer to the Long Island home where I grew up, closer to my parents, closer to my dearest friends—and closer, I thought, to the life I wanted to live.

I was thirty-nine years old. I was hoping to get married and start a family of my own. I was also still grinding. My job at the NFL Network was supposed to entail one column per week on NFL.com and roughly one appearance per week on the network's flagship show, *NFL Total Access*. Within no time, I was on TV every day. The network depended on me to be its news-breaker. I was writing stories every day. But the story I pursued hardest was my own.

My failed marriage was just one in a long list of failed relationships. I believed my luck would change when I moved to New York. Even before I moved in, I had a woman in my sights. We were introduced the same way I had met other women through the years, by mutual friends, thinking there might be some sort of love connection. So we exchanged emails for over a month, starting in January 2006, and we seemed to hit it off. Even though I had not physically met her, and there was so much about her that I didn't know, something about it felt magical.

I left the Pro Bowl in Hawaii in mid-February, flew straight to New York, and in the middle of the night, went right to the apartment I had rented on the Upper West Side. I was so excited to meet this woman in person that I had arranged for the doorman to let her in days before I even got there, so she could inspect and prep the apartment at her request.

When I walked into that empty apartment at about 1:00 in the morning, I found one of the nicest gestures I could ever imagine.

My new woman friend, whom I had not yet met, had left out chocolates for me, sprayed her perfume on my pillows, and laid a trail of rose petals all around the apartment. It truly took my breath away.

We met for the first time the very next night, a dinner date on the Upper West Side. That relationship started fast, sputtered out, and then, after a few weeks, reality set in. We dated for a short time, and then it ended.

If you want to know what went wrong with that woman and that relationship, here it is:

She was dating me.

I wanted a relationship to work out so badly that I painted this picture in my head of the perfect relationship . . . and every time imperfections surfaced, as they inevitably do, the relationship stalled. It wasn't anybody's fault but mine. What I failed to take into account at the time was that we're all imperfect. No relationship, or person, could live up to the standard I'd set in my mind.

It wouldn't have mattered if Michelle Obama had shown up at my front door. Or Jennifer Lopez. Or Olivia Munn. Whoever. Just name a woman you find charming, beautiful, and lovely, and understand—I would have found something wrong. I wouldn't like her legs, or her laugh, or what she ordered for dinner, or the way she cried, or the fact that she cried at all. My friends mocked me for it all the time.

A lovely, very nice schoolteacher was too soft-spoken—not enough energy. An attractive, alluring saleswoman said she didn't like that I worked on Sundays—and I couldn't do anything to change that, so that was the end there. Sometimes relationships would end over *nothing*. A mild disagreement. A bad moment. A wisp of air. As soon as something wasn't exactly as I'd envisioned, I bailed. It was over.

I made so many stupid decisions and silly mistakes. My relationships brought a rush, the same way breaking a big story would bring one. Then the high would wear off, and it would be time to move on to the next one. Sometimes I wondered if the mind-set I needed for work—go hard for twenty-four hours, before moving on to the next story—secretly seeped into my thinking and adversely affected my relationships. I'd meet a woman and I'd tell my friends, "Oh, this one's got a chance," just like a tip on a big story. Every time, I meant it, too. But my friends knew me better than I knew myself; they would just laugh at me. They knew the end was coming well before I did. They had seen it too many times—one bad rerun after another.

I wanted fireworks, and that's what I got: one spectacular, explosive moment, followed by everything going quiet and dark.

I was in a lot of relationships that were serious until they began.

I dated a lot of women when I lived in Denver. That sounds exciting, but it wasn't. I was not looking to be a lifelong bachelor. I lived what sounds like a great life in the rare times I wasn't working: Wake up, work out, play golf, go on a date. But it's only great if that's what you want. For me, it was definitely unfulfilling.

But there I was, a single man in New York, living in the same building as Howard Stern and NASCAR star Jeff Gordon. That also sounds a little better than it was—my six hundred–square-foot, one-bedroom apartment was a closet compared to theirs. But it was a clean, well-lit apartment. It was my New York City rental, and I loved it.

I was ready to live the life I envisioned, with my friends all around me. This was news to my friends. A lot of them lived in the suburbs and had children. They weren't able to—or even interested in—dropping everything to come hang out with a single guy who had lived in another state for two decades.

My search for a wife continued. I kept looking, kept hoping, kept dating, kept failing, kept sinking. One woman, who was on TV, stopped corresponding with me for two weeks, then called me and ask to go to a spinning class together. I said, "Yeah, OK." But I was really thinking, *What's going on here?* Another woman that I knew from college sent me a rather nondescript note about possibly getting together, then never followed up. This was how it went. Nothing caught, my mood sank, and now the new surroundings didn't look quite as appealing as they once did.

It only took me a couple of months to realize my life in New York was not what I'd expected. I started to think I may have made a mistake. It was such a foolish, simplistic plan: *I'm going to go home, surrounded by my friends and family, start a new social life, hopefully meet the perfect New York woman, and be happy.*

The low point came Memorial Day weekend, the traditional start of summer, one of the best social weekends of the year. I did not have a lot of social options in New York City, but my friend David Simon invited me out to his family's house in Southold, Long Island.

The train ride out there felt long and lonely. And when David picked me up at the train station in Hicksville to drive me out to Southold, I felt I might have been at my low point. Both he and his brother, Michael, tried to talk some sense into me at a time when they were dealing with some issues of their own.

Michael had been divorced twice. He had two kids. He was trying to find stronger professional footing. He kept listening to my sorrows, and he would say, "What are *you* worried about?" I knew what he meant—he had much greater responsibilities than I did. I was working for the NFL Network and living in

Manhattan. It seemed great from the outside, but when you're living in quicksand, you can't figure your way out. I was miserable.

I'd had some rough moments, like anybody else—seeing other relationships fail, struggling to find a job when I started my career. But this was the worst I'd ever felt. It felt like I was breaking down mentally and physically.

How bad did it get? Well, at one point, I literally stopped going to the bathroom, or at least . . . how do I put this gently? I couldn't do my full business in there. This lasted for more than a week, and I grew increasingly concerned.

Then, on the last day of May, I went to the gym, where I watched Katie Couric's last appearance on *The Today Show*. As she signed off from the show, it brought me to tears. Nothing against Katie Couric, but that was a bad sign. I headed to appointments with three therapists. Yes, three. In one day. They were like tryouts. I began cycling through them the way I would dates or stories. I was so desperate to feel better that I would have done anything.

The first therapist was OK. She said *The Today Show* touched on my emotions and I needed to give therapy a real chance. I didn't love her, but I wrote in my journal:

I do think I just liked having somebody to talk to at this point, I'm that desperate to feel better.

The second therapist was much more insightful. She had explained why my rose-petal romance was failing: It was built on fantasy. She said that I was impulsive, that I saw everything as black and white, and I needed to get myself under control.

After my second appointment, I ate a bagel and lox for lunch, hoping it would help my stomach. It didn't. I had high hopes for my third therapist of the day—in my personal journal that day, I described her as "my top candidate." But like in so many of my romantic relationships, my high expectations quickly led to disappointment.

Even at a time of mental and physical illness, I still found time to schedule another forgettable date that night, before going home. I don't even remember who the date was with, but I remember the rest of the night well. When I got into bed, the pain in my stomach was so debilitating that I knew I would end up in the hospital. My body was not functioning properly.

I took a taxi to Roosevelt Hospital. They asked me to rate the pain on a scale of one to ten. I gave it a nine. I was practically hyperventilating when they put in a catheter. Never had one of those before—and never want one again. Ever.

I wrote in my journal:

It hurt like a bitch and I was crying and I was lonely and I was scared.

I really didn't think much beyond that: *Lonely, scared, can't use the restroom properly.* I didn't even know whom to call. I felt totally alone. I had moved home, yet I felt completely and overwhelmingly lost. My life in New York had peaked the moment I saw those rose petals. From that point on, it had gotten progressively worse.

When I got out of the hospital, I met a woman on a bus. She said she was a model for commercials; she made me miss something I didn't even have. At the time, rain was coming down. I had an umbrella, but of course, it was too small and didn't work. I started cursing New York City, the place that was supposed to rescue me. I thought about how much I hated it and how miserable I was. Picture this, because it actually happened: I was standing on a corner, in the rain, with an umbrella that was too small, and a taxi whizzed past, through a puddle, and doused me. I was a real-life Charlie Brown—only more hopeless.

I didn't know what was left for me to do. There was no other place for me to go. I thought about going back to Denver, but it had only been a few months. So as difficult as it was to do, as much as I was contemplating yet another change, I decided to stick it out. I decided to stay in New York.

A month later, my friend Jeff Rubin called. He had the names of three women for me to call.

He said I could call any of the three, but he recommended that the first one I should call was a woman named Sharri Maio.

Before I called her, though, he told me there was something I needed to know: She was a 9/11 widow with a six-year-old son.

7

A 9/11 widow? Some men might have bailed as soon as they heard that piece of information. I knew that because, for a long time, I was one of those men.

But that was before I felt so lonely, before I ended up in the hospital in severe pain with nobody to call, and before my fortieth birthday was creeping up on me. I was not looking for the perfect résumé anymore. I had taken a hard look at myself.

I didn't love any of the three therapists I saw, but they all hit on the same themes: I had been focusing on the wrong things, and I put so much pressure on relationships that they burst. My mind was all over the place. Everyone was giving me names of women to meet.

So when Jeff asked if I still wanted to go out with Sharri, knowing she was a 9/11 widow with a son, I said, "Sure."

After Jeff mentioned Sharri, I happened to look through my journal entries from the previous year. I did it because I wanted

to figure out exactly how much work I had done for the NFL
Network since the start of the last football season, but the real
revelation had nothing to do with work. My entries about dating all read the same way. I summed them up in my journal:

> *There have been identical patterns of behavior.*
> *Amazingly so. Eerie.*

So that day, I did something amazingly unfamiliar. I picked
up the phone and called Sharri.

Sharri was insistent: Any man she dated had to know she was
a widow with a six-year-old boy. And they had to know how her
husband had died. It was like they were signing a waiver: *Yes,
I understand.* And it was nonnegotiable. She didn't want to sit
down for dinner and have to tell a man she had just met all
about her husband dying in a terrorist attack.

Almost five years had passed since Joe died. His parents,
Paula and George, had encouraged Sharri to start dating again,
and eventually she had. She had been on a lot of dates and in
one semi-serious relationship since Joe died, and she figured
that any man who dated her would have to be comfortable
with her past and embrace the idea of loving both her and
her son.

She had gone on one date with a man who had a daughter
with a visible disability, and he was hesitant to show Sharri a
picture of her. She was disgusted and wanted to go home. She
did not understand how anybody could be embarrassed by his
own child—or worried about how somebody would react.

As I called Sharri, I honestly wasn't sure how I felt. A widow with a six-year-old still didn't sound like my dream date. But I thought about all the times I had gotten my hopes up, then ended the evening paying for a nice dinner with a woman I knew I would never see again. It was such a waste. I'd be sitting there, thinking, *OK, how much longer do I have to stay here before I can get back to work?* I thought, *I'm done with that. Let's just see how we connect.*

Sharri and I talked on the phone for around an hour, and we connected right away, which was encouraging. There were other phone connections in the past, for sure, but this one did feel different. It felt natural, comfortable, not forced, though she did not take kindly to my first-date proposal. I suggested we go to a barbecue at one of my friends' houses—low-key, no romantic pressure. She said no chance. She had visions of turning around to put food on her plate, and behind her my friends would be holding up signs rating her:

"EIGHT!"

"SIX!"

"THUMBS-UP!"

"YOU CAN DO BETTER, ADAM!"

That wasn't my intention. My idea was more: "If I don't like her, I can hang out with my friends, and at least it will be a fun night." But she was adamant we go somewhere other than a friendly barbecue—either for coffee, lunch, dinner, but away from my friends. And so on July 9, 2006, I borrowed my sister's new car, which still had the new-car smell, and drove to Sharri's house on Long Island. These were the pre-GPS, pre-Waze days. Sharri had given me directions that led me right into her driveway.

The grounds looked like a botanical garden. There were flowers everywhere. The lawn was well manicured, and the house incredibly well maintained. The outside of the house had a cheer and warmth to it.

I parked my sister's car, walked up to Sharri's front door, and was greeted by another great sight: Sharri. I can still remember my eyes scanning her over from toe to head, tight khaki pants to black sweater, up to her face, and I was blown away. She was gorgeous. She showed me around her house, which was lovely. We continued talking, just like we did on the telephone. We clicked again.

I thought, *Yes!*

She thought, *He is wearing a tight long-sleeved orange shirt. Ugh.*

But she figured she could improve my wardrobe. She had the same thought I did: *This seems promising.*

We went out to this local American restaurant near her house. I later learned that Sharri liked to go on dates there because if they didn't go well, she could get home quickly. But this time, she didn't seem like she was in a rush. We sat in the corner, up against the window. The restaurant was crowded, but we felt as if we were in our own world. She ate her artichoke salad and chicken Milanese, I ate my mussels and yellowfin tuna, and we just talked.

I told her about my sister, Marni, and her husband, Mike, and my brother, Jordan. She told me about her sister, Robyn, and Robyn's husband, Jordan. We talked about our dating histories. We just laughed, had fun. It was easy. I was calling her Maio, her last name. She was calling me Schefter. We made a bet: Whoever called the other by his or her first name first would owe the other a dollar. It was pretty funny.

Sometimes you know a date is going well just because both of you order dessert. It doesn't always mean you *want* dessert.

You can always go home and pull some frozen yogurt out of the freezer. It means you want the date to keep going. Sharri ate an apple tart, I had berry pie, and we just kept talking.

We talked about her son, Devon, and her husband, Joe, and what it was like raising Devon without Joe. What Sharri had done was remarkably commendable to me. She was raising her son by herself, taking care of her home, doing it in a strong and independent way that attracted me as much as her appearance. None of this felt awkward to me. It wasn't storybook, but it was comfortable.

After dinner, we drove back toward her house. She said her in-laws were at the house, babysitting Devon, so we parked the car on the street and talked, touching on topics that spanned from family to friends to life.

She asked me when my birthday was.

"December 21," I answered.

She looked shocked. I thought it might be her birthday, too. It turned out to be Joe's birthday.

That was odd—not just because we have the same birthday but because it came up on our first date, at the moment when we were both thinking there might be some chemistry.

We kept talking about birthdays. She said Devon was born on June 21; that is my half birthday—and Joe's, of course—and the date my grandfather Poppy Marty died in 1968. Later we learned that my grandmother Nanny Blanche had the same birthday as Joe's grandmother Louise, who was known as Nanna Bubs. So that also felt odd. But Sharri and I got along great, talked for another thirty to forty-five minutes, and made plans to go out again Saturday night. I was pumped.

I kissed her in my sister's car, down the street from the house she shared with her late husband, in which her in-laws were sitting on the couch. I brought her home and watched her walk back to her house.

I drove away from Sharri's house after our first date thinking that I had found my future. It was only one date, sure. I didn't even know how to spell her name yet—I thought Sharri had only one *r*. But being with her just felt right. I drove back to my sister Marni's house in Melville and told her and her husband, Mike, how excited I was. At 11:00 P.M., I fell asleep in my nephew Casey's room with the TV on ESPN, watching a late-night *SportsCenter*. I woke up the next morning at 5:30, still feeling the fumes of excitement from the night before. That day, I wrote in my journal:

> *Even though I didn't get much sleep, it was one of the first peaceful mornings I've had in a while.*

And:

> *She made me happy. Or I made her happy. Or whatever. I was friggin happy!!!!*

I went for a walk with Marni and her friend Cari around their neighborhood. I talked about Sharri, and I told them about Sharri's ex-husband having the same birthday. Cari got chills.

I am an all-in guy. It's how I live my life. *Let's get things done.* It feels like it has helped me professionally. When there's breaking news, it's like a jolt of electricity. This was not entirely dissimilar to another kind of jolt with a different kind of adrenaline. So after that first date with Sharri, my primary thought was: *When do I call her?* I didn't want to seem overanxious . . . even though I was.

I left Marni's house and played golf with some friends. When I got off the course, I had two messages on my BlackBerry—each from a friend trying to set me up with another woman. I thanked them, but at that moment, I wasn't thinking about dating anybody else. I was thinking about Sharri.

I decided to call her that day at 4:00 P.M., the ideal time that I came up with in my mind. It wasn't too quick after the date, but it was early enough to show how interested I was. I thought, *If she's interested, she'll pick up or call me right back*. That was my experience with other women I had dated. So I called and left a message.

Sharri didn't call me back that day.

Or the next.

In my world, with instant news and deadlines and show-times, an hour can feel like a day, and three days can feel like a lifetime. I kept checking the phone and kept seeing no voice mails or texts. With each hour that passed, more disappointment and despair set in. I called my therapist and explained that I had been on a date and thought we'd hit it off, but then I'd called the woman and she hadn't called back.

My therapist said, "So?"

I said, "Well, how do you not call back if you like someone?"

She said, "Adam, you went out with this woman on one date. What are you picturing here? What was so perfect? Do you think this woman is just going to change your life? Why are you so upset and so worked up over one woman—who you just met—not calling?"

I was so consumed with finding a mate that I'd lost sight of the fact that people have lives. They don't move at the same hyper speed, in the same way, that I do. They don't attach a sense of urgency to many things. They can't act like their lives are breaking news, acting on it right away, no time to waste, this must get done now. This could wait. Relationships can wait. They need to breathe. This is true for everybody, but especially single moms, which I didn't really consider at the time. I didn't know any better. I was looking for a woman to build my life around. Sharri was looking for somebody who fit into her life. There was a difference.

My therapist said, "Why do you need that phone call to be happy? You're unhappy she didn't call back, and it's totally dictating your moods about everything in life." She was right.

Sharri does not move on things like I do. She is not on the phone all the time. She does not instantly respond to texts and emails. She responds when she's ready, whenever that is. Sometimes it's a few hours later; sometimes it's a few days later. But eventually she did call, and when she did, I was filled with happiness and excitement. It felt like validation.

I had big plans for our second date. My dating style was definitely *not* "Hey, let's get a burger and a beer." I always had big, detailed plans, going back to my college days at Michigan. I'd lay out this perfect night in Ann Arbor: Zingerman's Deli for dinner, then a Michigan hockey game, then a bar called Rick's for drinks, and my friends would make fun of me. They'd say, "Let life happen, man." But that wasn't my nature.

Before this second date, I actually walked around Greenwich Village and the Lower East Side, and scouted restaurants and tables like NFL teams do college quarterbacks. Finally, after visiting a half dozen restaurants, I settled on a plan.

I decided Sharri and I first would have drinks in the Time

Warner Center in Manhattan. Then we would go to an Italian restaurant downtown, Il Cantinori, which had beautiful flowers all over the place. Then, if all went well—and I was hopeful and confident it would—we would go back to my apartment on 67th Street, drink prosecco, and listen to music.

And that's what we did: Time Warner Center, Il Cantinori, back to my apartment. I put on the *Notting Hill* soundtrack on my CD player. I brought out a bottle of prosecco. I thought it was perfect. Romantic. Everything was going according to script.

But Sharri didn't bite. "So," she said with a high degree of skepticism, "how many girls have you done this for before?"

She scoffed and dismissed my plans, staying in my apartment long enough for me to give her a kiss goodbye, nothing more. I was starting to understand that Sharri Maio's head was not in the clouds next to mine. I was looking for a woman to marry; she already had been married. Her world revolved around her son. She was open to the possibility of marrying again, but she did not have her heart set on it.

I wanted somebody who had chemistry with me. Sharri needed somebody who had chemistry with her *and* Devon. Sharri would often let Devon meet the person she was going out with because she wanted to see the reaction. Not from Devon. Devon was a kid—however he reacted was fine. She wanted to see how her date reacted, whether the man was playful, uncomfortable, smiling, nervous, whatever.

I tried to build a relationship with Devon, too. Each time I visited from New York City, I brought him a little gift. One time it was a truck, another time a package of tattoos, which he loved. We each would put on the tattoos and wear them around for days. It was so important for me to try to make

Devon comfortable that I would do things with him that I wouldn't ordinarily.

The first time I introduced Sharri and Devon to my family, we went to the beach in Point Lookout. I never much liked swimming or going in the ocean, but that day, I took Devon in the ocean for a couple of hours, without getting out. When I finally did get out, my parents knew then that Sharri and Devon were different because they never had seen me stay in the ocean that long for anybody. But for Sharri and Devon, I was willing to do anything.

Devon was sweet and quiet, and we got along well. Sharri and I kept dating, with me taking more and more regular train trips from the city out to Long Island. Finally, after a month or so, I asked if I could leave some clothes at her house rather than having to schlep them back and forth from my apartment to her house on the train every time. I was tired of hauling a duffel bag around New York City.

Sharri lived in a nice-sized home. I asked for a drawer.

She broke up with me.

She viewed one drawer as an infringement on her space and life. She didn't want anyone in her house full-time while she was busy raising Devon. The next time she had a man in her home on a regular basis would be when there would be a full-time man in Devon's life—not any time before. Anyone who wanted a drawer got the boot instead.

Sharri had spent five years making that house her home. If she was wary of giving even a small piece of it to a man she had been dating for only a few weeks, who could fault her?

She had created a playroom for Devon. She hired landscapers. She covered the walls and ceiling of two bedrooms in fabric, softening them, making them as cozy and inviting as she possibly could.

Her parents would ask her, "When are you going to stop decorating?"

She had no answer. She was not prettying up the home just so it was pretty. She was prettying it up because she *liked* prettying it up. It comforted her. She liked having contractors and painters and construction workers in the house. She liked hearing their voices. It gave her an activity and a distraction, all at once. They provided company without the awkwardness that intimacy can bring. She wanted to keep redecorating until the house felt just right, even when she wondered if it ever would.

You can move things around a house. It's not so easy to rearrange a community. Sharri started to feel like an oddball in a homogenous town. She did not see widows or single moms. She wondered if she belonged. She had moved to this house to escape Manhattan. Now she found herself longing for the city, for its quirks and its diversity.

She put the house on the market again. As she stood there with the broker and a woman who was thinking of buying the house, the woman asked, "Are we allowed to paint over the mural?"

Sharri was hurt by the question. The mural was special to her. She thought the room was beautiful. She didn't understand why somebody would want to paint over it.

The broker said, "You can do whatever you want if you buy the house."

Sharri pulled the house off the market again. She kept living in the home she had bought with Joe, but her life, and the way she led it, had been split into two parts: One ended the morning of September 11, 2001, and one began September 12.

Before 9/11, she felt no connection to death; after 9/12, she felt permanently tethered to it. Before 9/11, relatives died, and she felt sad but still slightly removed from the devastation. After 9/12, she would hear stories about strangers dying and think, *That could be me.*

Before the attacks, Sharri was the woman who flew by herself to Japan, planning to live there for a while, assuming most Japanese people spoke passable English. They did not, but she enjoyed the experience anyway. She joined her husband on a work trip to Hong Kong, honeymooned in Italy, and lived in an emotional bubble, casually convinced that nothing bad would happen to her.

Starting on September 12, Sharri didn't even want to go from Long Island into New York City because she didn't want to be too far from Devon. She had lost one of the loves of her life and was terrified of not being there for the other.

Sharri was in a much more complicated emotional place than I was. She and Joe had dated for four years, and been married for three. She knew what it meant to be in a meaningful, life-affirming relationship. It wasn't like her marriage had ended in divorce and left her hoping for a fresh start. She was in no rush.

When she broke up with me, I was stunned. I had ended all those relationships for tiny reasons, and now I was losing another one over basically a drawer that she interpreted to mean more. I was devastated. I wondered why this was not working, what happened now, what I did now. Or what I didn't do. Whatever it was, I couldn't figure it out. I had a lot of questions, no answers.

I didn't call Sharri for three days, which was hard. I am someone who makes his living on the phone, who's on the phone all the time, with all sorts of people. I wanted Sharri in my life, badly, but still, I didn't call. I had been convinced—as hard as it was for me—that I needed to back off. It took everything within me to hold off from reaching out to her, to try to change her mind, to ask her for another chance.

I was restless. I had numbers of other women to call, so I began to mull over who I might have to call next if Sharri would not take me back.

But then, three days later, Sharri called and said three words that left me relieved and overjoyed.

"I miss you."

8

We started dating again, but I was still unsure if Sharri would break up with me again. And I was starting to get a fuller sense of what it meant to be a 9/11 widow. One day, soon after Sharri and I started dating, I reached out to Jon Frankel, who is a reporter for HBO's *Real Sports*. I called him because his wife, Erin, lost her husband, Greg, on 9/11. Greg Richards attended the University of Michigan at the same time I did and actually was one of my college fraternity brothers in Sigma Alpha Mu. He was younger than I was, but I remember him from our time together in the fraternity house. After he graduated, Greg worked for Cantor Fitzgerald and continued to work there, like Joe, until his death.

When I called Jon, I just wanted to see if there was some kind of magical formula that he would give to me that would help me along in this relationship, because I really wanted to make it work.

Jon was like me: He had a personal rule, before he met Erin, that he would not date anybody who had been married or had children. But also like me, he had been through some dating travails. Erin told him during their first phone call that she was a 9/11 widow, for the same reason Sharri told me right away: She knew that was a deal-breaker for some people. But Jon wasn't deterred. Nine months later, they got married.

I asked Jon if there was anything I should know about being with a 9/11 widow. He talked about being supportive and understanding. He did not say anything that really surprised me, but it was good to hear it from him. I'm a reporter—even if I know something is true, it's always comforting to hear somebody else confirm it.

When September 11, 2006, rolled around, I gave a lot of thought to how to handle it. It was the five-year anniversary of Joe's death. I knew it would be a painful day for Sharri, but this was still new territory for me.

When you are a 9/11 widow, everybody knows when it's the anniversary of your spouse's death. It's all over the news every year, especially in New York. And everybody seems to personalize it: *I remember where I was when the first plane hit.* It's natural, but it adds extra layers of difficulty to being a 9/11 widow.

I wasn't sure exactly how I was supposed to handle this. I sent Sharri a long email the night of September 10, hoping to hit the right tone. I wanted to convey how much I was thinking of her, and how hard I knew the day must be. I put a lot of thought into it. She sent me back one line, an indication of where her mind was at such a difficult time. I sent her flowers.

It was my first 9/11 since I had moved back to New York City, and I was struck by how different it was. The rest of the country knows that it is 9/11, but New York City feels it. I walked to my gym in Manhattan, and the streets seemed almost silent. It was so eerie.

As I lifted weights, I heard audio of somebody reading the names of all the people who had been murdered just five miles away. I hit the treadmill and then went home. I called the florist to make sure the flowers were being delivered, and I was told they were on their way. That afternoon, I got an email from Sharri:

> I LOVE MY FLOWERS! They are beautiful and they are just what I needed. I have a big grin on my face. Adding some levity to a tough day.

It affirmed that I had done the right thing, because at times like those, it's sometimes tough to figure out exactly what the right thing is. But the day was not over—on Long Island, Sharri was still trying to make her way through the day. Flowers and a nice email were not going to get her through it. I talked to her at around 6:00 P.M., and she seemed to be off in another world. It was the shortest conversation I could remember us having.

Romance can be easy. Relationships are hard. They require more complex chemistry. Many people wonder how they are supposed to know if they have met the person they are supposed to marry.

The first time that Joe's cousin Little Joe met Sharri, he heard Joe say that a girl they knew "got fat." Sharri snapped at him, "If you ever call a girl fat again in front of me, we're done."

And Little Joe thought, *Joe is going to marry her.*

Little Joe had seen enough of his cousin's girlfriends to know how most of them would react. They would say nothing, or they would eat salads for the next thirty meals so they could lose weight to impress Joe. They knew there were more women lining up to be with him. Sharri wasn't worried about that. She stood toe to toe with Joe. And Little Joe thought that, deep down, that was what Joe wanted. Joe Maio could have been a player, but he was a relationship guy—his friends all knew it, and he never tried to hide it. He wanted to be with a woman who respected herself.

Sharri and Joe broke up three times before they got engaged. They were in their twenties, still figuring out the requirements of permanent coexistence. Joe worked hard at it.

I was thirty-nine when I met Sharri. She had just turned thirty-seven. I don't think there is a right amount of time to date somebody before you commit. You have to do it until you're sure. I know people who dated for a week, got married, and are happily married twenty years later. And I know people who dated for five years, got married, and were divorced within a year. I think, no matter who it is, no matter how long you date, it's always a leap of faith. People change over time; they just do.

Sharri did not want somebody to wait on her hand and foot. She wanted somebody with some confidence. That's why, I learned later, when she broke up with me, *not* calling for three days was one of the best moves I had made. Sharri had seen my desperation and thought I was too eager to please. She saw that as a sign of weakness. When I didn't call, she thought, *Oh, he's not a pushover.*

One reason Sharri was attracted to Joe was that he was ambitious. She liked that quality. To her, ambition did not mean that he made a lot of money or had an impressive-sounding job.

She liked men who wanted something and went after it hard—whatever it was. It reminded her of her father, Chuck, a long-time Merrill Lynch employee who helped invent the original squawk box.

I'd like to think I have some of those same qualities that Joe and Chuck did. I am a workaholic by nature. It torpedoed a few of my previous relationships, but Sharri showed that she was drawn to ambition.

Within a few weeks of us getting back together, I felt very strongly that this was the right person for me. This wasn't just "I have a feeling about this." This was "I *know*. We've spent a lot of time together, and I know." Everything just flowed. Life was easier with each other than it was without each other.

I wanted to marry Sharri. I was ready to live together, but Sharri didn't want to live together unless we were engaged. She was extremely careful about dating with Devon around. She didn't want a man being around her house all the time if it wasn't serious. That added some urgency, but it was welcome urgency for me. I wanted to get engaged, too.

Before long, our engagement seemed inevitable. I heard her bring it up and talk about when we would get engaged, and I knew how decisive Sharri was. When she made up her mind, she would follow through; nothing was going to change her mind. We had a running joke. Sharri would say, "I want a ring big enough that I could eat off of." It was just her way of teasing me.

That December, I had to be in Pittsburgh for a Thursday night Browns-Steelers game on the NFL Network. I had done the sideline reporting for the NFL Network for the first Thursday night games it aired, with Bryant Gumbel as the play-by-play man and Cris Collinsworth as the analyst. I loved working with those guys and that Thursday night team. But the logistics surrounding it weren't always so pleasant.

Here is an example: The morning after the Browns-Steelers game, after not getting back to the hotel until about 1:00 or so in the morning, I woke up the next morning at 4:30 feeling the way most people feel when they have to wake up at 4:30 A.M. I checked out of my hotel and went outside, where it was dark and twenty degrees out. I had a flight to catch and a milestone moment ahead.

I had ordered the engagement ring, and the jeweler had told me the day before that it was ready. I was ready, too. I was still calling her "Maio," still referring to her as *Maio* in my daily journals, but I was in love. Still, the weight of the moment was starting to register with me.

Less than seven months earlier, I had gone to a hospital, so worn out, physically and emotionally, that I was unable to use a toilet. I was devastated by my inability to find a partner. Now here I was, on a plane from Pittsburgh to New York, preparing to propose.

I had picked this weekend for a reason. My fortieth birthday was that month, and one thing Sharri loves to do is to throw a party. I don't know anybody who does it better, from the food to the decorations to the entertainment. Sharri could be a party planner if she wanted. That's how good she is at it. So she planned to throw a fortieth birthday party for me at her house that Saturday night.

Without her having any idea, I wanted to turn it into an engagement party.

The plane's cabin was really cold—it felt like they had left it on the tarmac with the doors open all night. I fell asleep in my jacket. I woke up as we were circling New York. It was a bumpy flight, one of the worst I had been on in a long time. I started to feel physically ill.

We kept circling. I looked out and saw the World Trade Center.

Fitting, I thought.

And I said to myself, as documented in my journal entry that December day:

Joe, I'm going to be looking out for your family.

On the day Joe proposed to Sharri, he called his buddy Jeff Heitzner. "Can you meet me on the Upper West Side? I gotta talk to you." Jeff met him in a bar. Joe pulled out a bouquet of flowers and an engagement ring.

"You're getting married?" Jeff said. "That's awesome."

Joe was a bit nervous—not because he was worried he was making a mistake, and not because he was worried Sharri would say no. They had discussed getting married. The proposal would not come out of the blue. He was nervous just because this was one of those big milestone moments in life where even people like Joe Maio get a bit nervous. He wanted company. He had already brought the ring to Little Joe's apartment to show him.

Joe asked Jeff to hop in a limousine with him. Jeff thought it was funny; Joe wanted a wingman up to the eleventh hour.

As I went to pick up the ring and then meet Sharri, I felt the same way Joe must have felt when he proposed. The combination of a bumpy flight and butterflies in my stomach left me frantic. I got to my apartment and quickly packed for my trip out to Long Island. My mom called and told me the best route to take; she knew where I was going, but she did not know what I planned to do when I got there.

I picked up the ring in the Diamond District in New York; I even had my cousin Randy Penn, who lived on the Upper West Side, come with me to inspect it. I wanted a woman to see it before I presented it to the woman I wanted to marry. When Randy saw it, she gasped. She loved it. I thanked her for the support and got in a taxi as I headed out to Sharri's house. She came outside when I arrived, and I was so excited to see her that I wanted to propose right then and there, but I knew I had to wait. I had to hold back. I had a plan.

We went over to Devon's school. I was his show-and-tell project for the day. I met the kids and recommended they eat their fruits and vegetables and talked to them about being everything they wanted to be. Sharri sat in the back, smiling.

That night, I sent Sharri out for a massage while I stayed home with Devon. He was six years old at the time. I had decided to take Sharri's teasing about the size of the ring all the way to the end. I had purchased two rings: a really cheap one with a stone of cubic zirconia that was so small you could barely see it, and then the actual diamond.

On our drive home, I was so amused about my cubic zirconia plan that I actually started laughing out loud.

"What's so funny?" Sharri asked.

"Uh . . . you crack me up," I said.

Later that afternoon, while Sharri was out getting a massage, I had to rehearse everything with Devon, make sure he understood what was happening and the gravity of it. I showed Devon one of the rings.

"Are you going to marry my mom?" he asked.

"I'm hoping to," I said.

We rehearsed his part so that he had it perfected by the time Sharri got home. And when she did, I approached her with a gift in hand.

"I have something to show you," I said.

And with that, I gave her the cubic zirconia ring.

She looked at it, looked genuinely excited, and said, "Oh, I love it. I love it." And she did, sincerely. Had that been the ring, she would have said yes and thought nothing more of it.

But then I had Devon walk out of the kitchen and into the lobby to serve up the real ring—on a big silver platter. On the platter, surrounding the wrapped box, was a fork and a knife, and Sharri looked at Devon and the platter, totally confused. Then she opened the box on the platter and had a similar reaction to the first, with more tears, more hugs, more kisses, more emotion.

The real ring wasn't big enough for her to eat off of, which was what she'd requested, but she really didn't care how big the ring was. She was just happy she had found her second husband.

My fortieth birthday party that night would turn into an accidental engagement party. People came for my birthday and wound up celebrating our engagement. Sharri had invited a bunch of my friends from Colorado, and it was fitting to have them there, because they had witnessed my dating follies up close. One friend who flew in was Rick Reilly, one of the greatest sportswriters ever—first with *Sports Illustrated*, then with ESPN. He was a guy I idolized. Rick lived in Colorado and was always so nice to me. I used to tell him if there was anything he ever needed, to call me. Then one day I was on vacation in Aspen and he called me.

He said, "Remember you said if I needed anything, you could help?"

I said, "Yeah."

"Can I stay at your place?"

"Yeah. When do you want to stay here?"

"Can I be there tonight?"

He was in the process of getting divorced. I drove back from my vacation to let him into my house, to get him set up.

Now Rick was there for my engagement. He knew how badly I wanted to get married and have my own family. We had talked about it a lot. So he found this all hilarious: I moved to New York, and within a year, I had a wife, a six-year-old, and three dogs. He said it was like Sea-Monkeys, the old at-home hatching kit for brine shrimp. Instant family.

The party was fantastic. Food and candles were everywhere, everyone laughing, everyone having a great time. My family and friends were there, Sharri's family and friends were there, and it was the first time our extended lives were all placed together. I remember thinking that if I had known how much happiness and fun everyone would have, how much joy and excitement I would feel, I would have proposed after six weeks of dating Sharri instead of six months. It felt that good and that right.

But before the party even began, we had one phone call to make.

Sharri called George Maio. I had gotten to know Paula and George a bit in the few months that I had been dating Sharri, and we got along really well. From the first time I met them—and I was more nervous to initially meet them than to meet Sharri's parents—they could not have been any more welcoming or gracious to me. They treated me as if I were marrying one of their own children, which in a way, I was. George was pleased that Sharri had fallen in love again, and he saw that Devon and I were building our own strong relationship. He liked that, too.

George was at Adios Golf Club in Coconut Creek, Florida. The course was designed by Arnold Palmer, and a lot of famous, tough men were members: Dan Marino, Cris Carter, Carl Yastrzemski, people like that. George was a member, too.

After Sharri told Paula and George the news, they each asked to speak to me. I was really moved by that. Paula said she had seen the spark return to Sharri for the first time in five years. I didn't know what to say. I just thanked her. I handed the phone back to Sharri, who spoke to Paula and George.

"Devon wants to speak to you," Sharri said.

She gave the phone to Devon and told him George was on the line. He was so excited.

"Poppy! Poppy!" Devon said. "I'm gonna have a daddy!"

After they hung up, George walked straight into a restroom and cried.

9

A few months after Joe Maio died, Sharri got a phone call: they had found Joe's Cantor Fitzgerald ID card. The plastic badge was in perfect condition, except for a little warping.

Not long after that, two police officers came to Sharri and Joe's house. Sharri answered the door. She understood, instinctively, why they were there.

They had found Joe's remains.

She went to a funeral parlor and saw the body bag. It was as tall as Joe was. She was confused. Hadn't his body been destroyed in the building? Had he jumped when he couldn't take the heat and smoke?

"How did he die?" she asked. "What happened to him?"

They wouldn't tell her.

The Maio family held a funeral in Rockland County, New York, and they buried Joe.

What did the ID card and body bag mean? We still don't know. George thought the fact that the ID badge was intact meant he had jumped. He thought Joe saw some of his colleagues die and so he leaped from the building.

In a way, it doesn't really matter exactly how Joe died— whether he stayed in the building or jumped as dozens of others did. He was killed because terrorists hijacked planes and flew them into his building. But it's natural to wonder how a loved one spent his final minutes.

In some cases, the speculation may even say something about how people saw Joe.

Sharri could not imagine Joe jumping—the Joe she knew would never have abandoned his colleagues in the building. She thought he would stay with them until the end. Jordan Bergstein kept imagining that Joe jumped because Joe believed he could land safely and walk away. This was illogical, but it was what Jordan wanted to believe. Joe was such a positive person. Says Jordan, "I like to think he had hope the whole way down."

10

I had hope the whole way in. All those years, I had imagined I would meet the right woman. I didn't know where or when, but I believed it. Now the details had come into focus. I was excited to begin my new life.

As soon as Sharri and I got engaged, I moved into her and Joe's house.

Sharri wondered if it would be awkward for me to live in the house she had bought with Joe. For the second time since he'd died, she thought about selling it, but I did not feel uncomfortable there. I felt like I was home, and I deferred to her, as I've tried to do on many things in life. Whatever made her comfortable, whatever she wanted. She decided not to sell it.

Devon had grown so much from the boy who would excitedly greet his father when he came home from work. He had gone from sleeping in a crib to sleeping in a bed, and he developed this habit of sleeping in Sharri's room. He would climb into her bed, play with her hair, and fall asleep.

Devon was fifteen months old when Joe died, but he was six when I met him. That meant he was too young to remember his father, but he was old enough to understand I was a new person in his life.

It wasn't enough to tell Sharri, "I understand you have a child, and I am OK with it." I had to form a connection with Devon, but I didn't know how, and I did not assume he wanted me there. Sharri worried he would be jealous when I moved in, but he really wasn't. He adjusted quickly.

Still, I put in my best effort to make him feel like I was like a dad. My instinct was to bond with him over sports. I think it's a natural thing for a lot of fathers and sons. It's something you can talk about, something you can share. You watch a ball game. You play catch. You talk about whether the Knicks will ever be good again.

When I was a kid, I was a huge sports fan, and it was the most real and palpable connection I had with my father. We always could talk about the Jets or Giants, the Yankees or Mets, the Knicks or Nets, the Islanders or Rangers, or his college team, Penn State. I carried that with me into adulthood. But Devon was not a huge sports fan. He didn't hate sports, but they weren't his favorite thing. You can't make someone love sports any more than you can make him love art or architecture or classical music. So we had to find other ways to connect.

When Sharri and I were dating, I would bring him toys and temporary tattoos. It was a very different experience for me and not the kind of courtship I ever could have envisioned. I had to find non-sports activities and topics that interested him. I had started this relationship with Sharri with a bottle of prosecco and the *Notting Hill* soundtrack, and here I was, bringing temporary tattoos to a boy and helping his mom pick him up from elementary school.

This sounds like a romantic comedy. At times, I wished it felt more like one.

When I was single, my days often revolved around two things: work and eating. The work does not require much elaboration: I tried to break stories, cover unique angles, carve out my place in the NFL reporting world, first as a Broncos beat writer and then as a league insider for the NFL Network. I took pride in my work. Every trade or free-agency signing was a way to be judged and measured. I never wanted to fall short.

As for the eating, I'll lay it out simply for you: I am not one of those people who can grab a grocery store bagel for breakfast and have a granola bar for lunch and eat whatever happens to be in the fridge for dinner and be happy. I like good, healthy, satisfying meals—not necessarily pricey meals, just something I actually *want* to eat. If I don't have that, I sometimes can get grumpy.

Sharri is not like that. Food is as important to her as handbags are to me. And for that first year or two, we both had to adjust to what the other needed—and we had to do it while raising a child.

Devon and I had at least one thing in common: Devon loves eating. He just loved to dive into something good, especially desserts. He never would miss a dessert. He acted as if there were laws that required it. There is an old line about somebody who "never missed a meal," and it was literally true of Devon.

I had been subletting my town house in Denver when I met

Sharri. After we got engaged, I sold it and with that money bought a house in Sag Harbor, out near the Hamptons. One night, we were driving back from Sag Harbor and Devon fell asleep in the car. This wasn't surprising; it was 11:00 P.M., and he had spent all day swimming in the hot sun. So after we got home, I got him out of his car seat, carried him upstairs to his room, and tucked him in.

And then, at three in the morning, he woke me up.

I said, "What's going on?"

He said, "I didn't get to have dinner."

It was so funny. He didn't say, "I'm hungry." He said, "I didn't get to have dinner." It was like he'd missed an appointment and felt this urgent need to make up for it. *I had something I was supposed to be doing and I didn't do that and so I need to do that. Now.*

I loved Devon from the beginning, and we had a lot of great times, but now that I look back on it, I'm not sure how prepared I was to be an instant dad. Even physically, I wasn't prepared. My body was not used to being around kids. My immune system wasn't ready for the runny noses and the poorly washed hands. I am fortunate that I have generally been a healthy person in my life, but that first year that I lived with Sharri and Devon, I must have gotten twenty colds. I was sick all the time—nose running, eyes watering, throat itching. My body just kept breaking down.

Together, Sharri and Devon and I tried to mold a new life for ourselves, but we weren't entirely sure how to do it. My life and Sharri's life were completely different in ways I didn't really understand, even though they were right in front of me. I was comfortable with the *idea* of dating a widow with a son, but I didn't fully appreciate the reality of what it was like to be a parent. I had never done it. Sharri's whole life revolved around Devon—as it should have—but that was a huge adjustment for me.

Reality smacked me in the face on a daily basis. I couldn't just go to the gym when I woke up. I couldn't have a sit-down dinner every night. I couldn't do what I wanted when I wanted. I wasn't the only person to worry about anymore; Sharri and Devon were. There were adjustments to make every day. Just as you can't build a marriage entirely on sweet gestures like prosecco and flowers, you can't get a child to view you as a parent simply by bringing him gifts.

Friends saw me with Devon and thought, *If you didn't know the backstory, you would assume that was his son.* My transition appeared seamless to them, but it didn't always feel that way to me.

Our personalities were different. I am always moving, always working. Devon is much more laid-back. Sharri felt like I didn't compliment him enough. She took it personally. I made mental notes to improve the ratio of compliments to criticism. I also had to understand what it was like for Sharri. She was naturally protective of him and wanted nothing but the very best for him. She also always felt bad that he'd missed out on so much, and she wanted it made up to him in any and every which way possible.

I found myself experiencing some of the same problems with Devon that I'd had with other relationships: I went in expecting perfection, and when I failed to find it, I struggled to adjust. I wanted to make it perfect, and sometimes that made it worse.

I am a "glass half-full" person, and Sharri is more "glass half-empty." She grew up in a house with a conservative, levelheaded father. She does not fall for big promises. When I tell her something great will happen, she says, "Don't say that. Things happen in life. They don't always go the way you think they will."

She believes you have to be yourself in a relationship. You can increase your awareness and sensitivity toward the other person, but you can't change who you are. I was still trying to navigate through that. It took some time.

The public moments, when you pick up a child from school or take him to the park, were easy for me. The private ones were more challenging. It was hard to discipline a child who didn't look at you as his natural father. It's hard enough to be a parent, but in many ways, it's even more challenging to be a stepparent. We both full well knew that, as hard as I tried, and as much as I did, Devon's real dad was, and always would be, Joe Maio.

I pushed forward in this new, unconventional, uncharted relationship. It wasn't always easy, but it always felt right.

On the morning of June 24, 2007, my sister, Marni, called. She asked if I was excited. I should have been; Sharri and I were getting married that day. The wedding was at Engineers Country Club on Long Island. This was the club that Joe had planned to join for the 2002 season. Sharri became a social member there; Joe never did.

And the truth is that, when Marni called, I wasn't excited, and I wasn't really nervous. It felt like just another day, which I interpreted as a sign of how right it was. I woke up in the same house and I watched Devon play racing games in the playroom.

The momentousness of the day did not really hit me until Devon told me, "I can't wait to give away my mom to you."

That went right into my journal. That touched me.

Then I started to get him dressed, and the day really started to feel different. He looked so cute in his little tuxedo. It took me six tries to get his tie on before I finally did it properly. It was the first time I ever saw Devon wear a tie, and having to put it on him symbolized the added responsibility that now was a welcome part of my life. I felt like a man who was about to get married—and also be Devon's dad.

By that afternoon, I had reached a stage of full-on nervousness. My hands were cold and clammy. I reached for the right words to say to Sharri. I told her I was honored to be marrying her, which was a weirdly formal thing to say and kind of awkward.

Devon walked his mom down the aisle. Sharri looked beautiful, Devon looked so handsome, and the day I thought might never come now was a reality.

Before I took Sharri's hand at the chuppah, I walked over to Devon, lifted him up, and gave him a big kiss. It must have touched everybody in the room, because you almost could hear a collective *Awww*. Everybody, I assumed, knew the circumstances of our lives.

We had a traditional Jewish wedding, and after we stepped on a glass to break it, a Jewish tradition, I cracked that it was "the last time I get to put my foot down."

The day was perfect in every way—perfect weather, a great reception. A lot of people from all aspects of my life were there—Mitch Albom, my mentor when I was a young journalist; former Broncos coach Mike Shanahan, who helped teach me about life in the NFL; my college buddies from Michigan, my parents' friends. Julie Romanowski, the wife of my friend and former NFL linebacker Bill Romanowski, grabbed the microphone from one of the band members at one point and sang "Wonderful Tonight," the Eric Clapton song.

We even discovered, randomly, that two of Sharri's parents' friends had known my parents when I was young. They saw my parents at the ceremony and thought, *What are* they *doing here?* They just thought they were going to Sharri Setty Maio's wedding. They hadn't realized the Schefter that she was marrying was the son of the Schefters they knew from life in Bellmore, New York. They joked that they could have introduced us twenty years ago.

Several guests told me I had a permanent grin on my face. It was true. I was so happy, and so appreciative of how much my life had changed. Hearing us introduced as Mr. and Mrs. Schefter was a "Wow!" moment for me.

I was not nervous for my toast. I talk for a living. And I figured, I just had to follow Devon, who had turned seven years old three days before our wedding. I didn't think it could be that hard; Devon was a quiet kid, not overtly outgoing. Not only that, but he had refused to let *anybody* help him with his speech. Sharri's mother tried, but he kept telling her, "Don't worry, Nanny, I can do this. I can do this." He wanted to do it all on his own.

Then he got up there and said, "Hello, everybody."

The whole crowd laughed and clapped. Pleasing a crowd is pretty easy when you are an adorable seven-year-old in a tux, holding a microphone.

Devon spoke from the heart.

"I am very lucky to be here today for my mom's wedding,"

he said. "I love my new dad. I'm just . . . thanking my mom . . . for marrying Adam."

The room melted. Sharri could not believe her shy son had stood up in a room full of two hundred–plus people and said something so sweet, all on his own.

It was just the kind of thing Joe would have done.

Then I got up to speak. I told our friends and family that, following Devon, "I never thought I would have big shoes to fill, but I do." I meant it. I told a story about our first date and gave what I thought was a pretty good toast. I thanked my family. And Sharri's family. And Joe's family.

When it was over, after the dancing and dinner and cake and ice cream and all the compliments over the flowers, I rode home with my new wife and our son. As we pulled toward our house, I could hear opera music coming from a nearby party.

It had been a wonderful, emotionally powerful day. And I had not even personally experienced all of it.

I found out later that at one point during the wedding, a few friends wandered out to the bar. These were people who knew Sharri and Joe, long before anybody could imagine Sharri and Adam. The friends talked about our wedding, and they seemed happy that Sharri had found love again.

Then there was a pause, and one of our guests said, "Let's not forget Joe, though. Joe's in this room, too." And they had a toast, at our wedding, to Joe Maio.

11

Six months before he died, Joe Maio asked his friend Jordan Bergstein to come visit his office in the World Trade Center.

Joe and Jordan were close friends and golf buddies who bonded over their love for action and the quick bursts of adrenaline that led to harmless highs. A lot of the action came in the form of gambling. Not high-stakes gambling, where the loser wonders how he will pay the mortgage. Mostly, they made small bets for their own entertainment.

Joe used his business acumen to make a betting market for the New York Jets, just among his friends. How many games would they win in the next four weeks? He traded positions with people and played the market well enough that he was sure to come out ahead, no matter what the Jets did.

Joe and Jordan bet when they were on the golf course. They even bet when they walked down the street. One of them would take out a nickel, point to a parking meter twenty feet away, and say, "Five dollars if you hit it."

From there, negotiations would begin.

"That's far. I want three-to-one odds."

"No. Straight up. You take the shot if you want it."

"Two-to-one."

"Deal. No tears."

"No tears."

That's how they always settled on the terms: *No tears.* It meant that all terms were final. No complaining later. And if you had asked them who won more bets, you would get firm answers: Joe would say *Joe*, and Jordan would say *Jordan*.

So here was Jordan Bergstein, on a cold, rainy day in the spring of 2001, only a few months after George W. Bush had taken the oath of the presidency and given his inaugural address:

> *Through much of the last century, America's faith in freedom and democracy was a rock in a raging sea. Now it is a seed upon the wind, taking root in many nations.*

Jordan rose up to the top of One World Trade Center in an elevator that traveled at a rate of 1,600 feet per minute. That elevator could make you forget how high you were going until you walked out and saw where you ended up.

Joe's childhood friends were amazed that Joe ended up working in the World Trade Center, of all places. They were amazed because when Joe was a child, he had one big fear:

He was scared of heights.

He did not hide this from anybody. He did not share it with

one friend and beg that friend to keep the secret. That wasn't his style. He was Joe Maio, take him or leave him. All his friends knew he was scared of heights.

When you're a child, getting to know your landscape, tunnels and ponds and spooky houses have an outsized hold on your mind. For Joe, the spot that messed with his head was a bridge near his house, in Spring Valley, New York, just over the New Jersey border.

The bridge was on Scotland Hill Road. It was an overpass over the Garden State Parkway; it was only as long as the width of the parkway and just high enough to allow trucks to pass through underneath. Joe and his friends had to go over this bridge to get to the Nanuet Mall on their BMX bikes.

Everybody else could ride their bikes across the bridge and think nothing of it. Whenever Joe rode to the bridge, he stopped, got off his bike, and walked it across. He would put his head on a friend's shoulder and hide his eyes so he would not even *glimpse* the edge of the bridge. Even if his friend started looking over the edge, Joe would freak out.

When he was little and walked past a high building, he would have to stay close to the building or he would get scared. He did not like standing on high balconies. When he visited his grandmother in Florida, the high steps and catwalks in her apartment complex frightened him. When he drove into the city, he had to be driving. He had to feel like he was in control. Otherwise, he would get nervous and worry about veering off the bridge and into the river.

This fear of heights was limited—he was fine, for example, on a chairlift or on top of a ski slope—but it was severe, and it extended into adulthood. He and Sharri once went hiking on

Victoria Peak in Hong Kong, and Sharri noticed he was a ghostly white.

He looked at her and said, "Can we go down now?"

But when Joe worked for Cantor Fitzgerald, in one of the tallest buildings in this country, on one of the highest floors in America, it felt different. He was enclosed. It felt safer. He would put his head against the glass and look out at the world below, unfazed. There was nothing to fear, no edge from which to fall. He was in an enormous office building. The windows were closed. Nothing could possibly happen.

Every once in a while, a friend of his from childhood would remember his fear of heights and ask what it was like working so high up in the World Trade Center.

"Bro," Joe would say, "I'm sitting on top of the world."

On this day, Jordan got out of the elevator. This was not a social visit. Jordan sold Joe disability and life insurance, and Joe had referred Jordan to a lot of his friends and colleagues at Cantor Fitzgerald. Joe even coached Jordan on how to sell to businesspeople. He'd say, "They're not interested in a long conversation. Think about what you want to say and say it. Don't beat around the bush."

Jordan had been in One World Trade Center a few dozen times to sell insurance, but this day felt different. It was stiflingly hot inside the building. The rain and fog meant he couldn't see outside. He was sure he felt the building swaying. It made him uncomfortable.

"This is scary, being up here," Jordan told Joe. "Do you ever think about how high you are?"

Joe said, "Never . . . until recently."

He explained that Cantor Fitzgerald was planning to move

its offices to New Jersey. Joe had started to think about the move.

"I gotta tell you," Joe said, "for the first time, I can't wait to go. I've had it, working up here."

12

Sharri and Joe had honeymooned in Italy. Sharri and I looked for places we could go on our honeymoon without getting on a plane. Joe's death instilled a lot of anxiety in Sharri. Initially, there was the anxiety of leaving her house and the anxiety of going back inside. She was terrified of losing Devon and scared to drive over a bridge into New York City. But maybe the biggest, most lingering fear, for her, was the fear of flying.

It's amazing how a fear can plant itself inside you in an instant and put down roots. Sharri never had a fear of flying before Joe died. She thought nothing of long transoceanic flights. But after 9/11, the image of those planes flying into the towers was difficult to shake. Anyone would understand.

So instead of flying, we went to Nantucket and Vermont for four nights. Sharri couldn't bear the idea of being away any longer. We had a great time. Devon stayed with Sharri's parents, and she knew he would be fine, but she worried anyway. Sharri was still so scared that something would happen to her and leave Devon an orphan. She couldn't get past it.

When we returned home, my adjustment continued. Getting married did not immediately make living together easier. That first year was rough for both of us. I had no idea what our married life would really be like. I thought I did, but I didn't. How could I know? I wanted romance, passion, love. I got that, but I also got everything else that comes with daily life.

Rick Reilly's Sea-Monkeys joke was hilarious at the time, but it was just a joke. Real life was not so simple. I was used to eating out for every meal; I'd been a bachelor. People talk about bachelors like they can date anybody whenever they want, but the real freedom is that you don't have to do anything. You can do whatever you're in the mood to do. Life with a spouse and a child doesn't work like that.

I'd ask, "Where are we going to lunch today?"

And Sharri would say, "What do you mean? I've got to get Devon from school, I have the plumber coming over . . ."

It was an enormous adjustment for me. My life changed quickly. I thought I was ready for it, but I really wasn't. I'd spent two decades as an adult basically doing whatever I wanted as long as I got my work done. Work was all that mattered, my only real concern. All of a sudden, I'd hear, "I know you have this story you're trying to break, but Devon is throwing up. We have to go to the doctor." I had this naive guy notion that it was going to be like dating: dinner dates, traveling—the life I had led, plus a partner. But when there is a child involved, it doesn't work like that. And we didn't have that typical break-in period to be together before a child came into the

picture. Devon was in the picture before I was. *I* was intruding on *their* world.

I had been living in a Denver neighborhood with plenty of
restaurants and bars. I'm not a big drinker—in fact, Sharri still
has never seen me intoxicated—but I enjoyed the social scene.
Then I moved to New York City. I was very lonely, but I was
still in *New York City*, by myself, living in a one-bedroom apartment, doing whatever I wanted to do. I was missing a lot of
things in life, but I did have social freedom.

Then I started living in a house in the suburbs with a wife,
a child, three dogs, and the memory of Joe.

He wasn't physically there, but he was always present.

Almost anybody who knew Sharri knew that he had lived
there. And those who didn't know Joe's story still figured she
had a husband there. One time she had gone into a restaurant
on a date, and the maître d' looked at the guy and said, "Hi,
Mr. Maio, how are you this evening?" She had been there so
often that he just assumed the man with her was her husband.
This was the same restaurant where Sharri and I went on our
first date.

I got used to people calling me "Mr. Maio"—when solici-
tors called our house, or came to the door, or stopped us in a
local shop. When they didn't know any different, I was Mr. Maio,
always.

I had moved into Joe's house. He had paid for it with money
from the job where he was working when he died. This is the
place where he would take baths with Devon until his hands
were wrinkly. His pictures were in frames on the shelves.
Sharri's redecorating projects continued, but still, if you thought
about it at all, it was hard to escape the feeling that he was supposed to be there.

I even inherited some of Joe's friends. Even though Joe and Sharri were a couple, some of his friends were not really Sharri's friends—they were just her husband's friends that she had met. Even some people who had been very close to Joe did not know Sharri that well. But some of his closest friends, like Jordan Bergstein, would become close friends of mine. It was just one more connection to the life of Joe.

Adjusting to my new world was hard enough, but it was important to make sure I remained sensitive to Sharri's thoughts and feelings about Joe, and both respected and honored his memory in my own way.

I tried to get to know Joe Maio as best I could. He couldn't just be Sharri's deceased ex-husband; I had to have a sense of who he was. I found out that we had some things in common. He was competitive, a trait I recognized. Sharri remembers playing Monopoly with him one Christmas, and he was hoarding so much real estate that she quit the game. At a blackjack table in Las Vegas, he once told her to move away. She was covering her eyes, and he said that was bad luck.

Joe set high professional goals and worked hard to achieve them, and I'm the same way. That torpedoed a few of my relationships, but not this one.

My workaholic tendencies and the 24-7 nature of my job meant that I was not always available at conventional times. Sundays always were for work. Holidays often took me away from her and the family. Night shifts often were regular shifts. And with the changing nature of the reporting job and the emergence of social media, no conscientious reporter ever was able to truly punch the clock, not anymore, not in this day and age. A reporter always is on the clock.

But Sharri was used to being alone. And no matter how much I worked, no matter how often I was gone, she would never feel as alone as she did in the days after 9/11.

13

I had worked at newspapers for a long time. Good stories always resonated. When I found out Joe and I had the same birthday, it made me feel as if Sharri and I were supposed to be together—which was great, because I already had seen and heard and felt enough to know I wanted us to be together.

But as we went from first date to married couple, I learned that this was not just a quirky fact or an eerie coincidence. It made my birthday a pretty odd day on the calendar for us. Even when you're an adult, your birthday is the one day of the year that is a celebration of you—a reminder of people who care about you, and a day to reflect and indulge yourself. But it's not that simple for us.

Every year on my birthday, I call my wife's deceased husband's parents to say I'm thinking of them. It's a strange tradition, but it's also the right thing to do. It's a hard day for Paula and George. I want them to know I will never forget that—or forget him.

And every year on my birthday, there is a part of my wife that's just a little bit distant. She doesn't really talk about it. She understands it's my birthday, and she doesn't want to spend it in mourning. I think, in some way, it helps her that my birthday is the same as Joe's—it gives her something to enjoy instead of just being sad all day.

I guess the best way to say it is this: Joe's birthday is easier for her because it's also my birthday. My birthday is complicated for me because it's also Joe's birthday. But every year, it has gotten a little easier for Sharri. There will always be some sadness for her on that day, as there should be. It might not be quite as pronounced as it was when we first met, but no matter what the celebration is on December 21, Joe is not far from any of our thoughts.

When I was younger, I occasionally felt pangs of jealousy. An ex-girlfriend would date somebody else, or somebody I found attractive turned out to have a boyfriend. But I can honestly say I have never been jealous of Joe Maio. I always have admired, respected, and appreciated him. I never have felt like I'm being compared to Joe, nor am I trying to live up to Joe. I don't know if that's normal or not, but Sharri's relationship with Joe never made me uncomfortable.

I guess this is partly because the Maios have been incredibly kind and decent and very accepting. I'm sure that made all of this that much easier. If they had been standoffish, or if they kept talking about how Joe was a better golfer or smarter businessman than I was, then maybe I might feel differently.

The only time I really get a jolt, and it's only a slight jolt, is when I hear Sharri call people on the phone and say, "Hi, this is Sharri Maio." Maio was not her maiden name; it's the name she had when she was married to somebody else. I think of her as Sharri Schefter, but she rarely calls herself Sharri Schefter. She still uses the last name Maio more than she does Schefter, in part because it is just one more way to be as connected as possible to Devon.

Sharri and I don't talk about Joe constantly, but we don't avoid talking about him, either. Sometimes, while we are hanging out as a family, she thinks about Joe—something he used to do, or a funny experience they shared, but Sharri is the only one in the family who has memories of him.

And so she looks at her husband and children, all happy and unimpeded by grief, and she thinks, *Maybe I shouldn't say this.*

And then she thinks, *No. This is my life. I can say it if I want to say it.*

I never try to stop her from talking about Joe. I never wince. Joe is a part of her, as well as a part of us. When we sit in our kitchen, I can't ask her to put her memories of Joe in a box in the attic.

Most days, we just try to live our lives, like anybody else does, but the reality is that in any relationship, two people come from two different places. In our case, Sharri was a widow with a young child, and I was a single man looking to get married and have kids.

My dream scenario always involved having children. That is what I pictured: find the perfect woman, get married, have kids. I had embraced the fact that the perfect woman for me was a widow with a son. I loved them both. But there was this difference between Sharri and me: She already had a biological child, and I didn't.

Her pregnancy with Devon had not been the smoothest—she

had been diagnosed with gestational diabetes, and he was a big baby: ten pounds, four ounces when he was born. Then, about a year after 9/11, Sharri was diagnosed with type 1 diabetes. I think of that as another consequence of 9/11. Doctors probably never will be able to prove this, but I believe the stress she experienced of being alone and having to raise a child by herself contributed to her body breaking down and the type 1 diabetes taking hold. Her diabetes is such a prominent part of our life. It had an impact on how she thought about having another child. She had already been through so much. She wasn't convinced she wanted to have more children.

She asked me, "What if we don't have another child? Will that be a deal-breaker for you? Because it might not happen."

I said, "I love you. Whatever you want is fine with me."

I meant what I said. I wanted another child, but I had learned by that point to appreciate what we had instead of focusing on something else I might want. We sort of tabled the discussion. There was never a definitive "let's try" or "no way." I figured we could make a final decision when we wanted. It didn't quite work out that way.

In February of 2008, I flew from New York to Indianapolis for the NFL Scouting Combine. As I landed, I had something happen to me that never had happened before and hasn't happened since. The moment I landed, I turned on my phone, and as soon as it turned on, it was ringing. It was Sharri.

I said, "Hello."

She said, "I'm pregnant."

I said, *"Pregnant?"*

There was surprise in my voice, concern in hers. She had

taken a pregnancy test, and it was positive. I couldn't quite believe it. It didn't make much sense to me.

We weren't *trying* to have a baby. We also weren't trying to
not have a baby. We were . . . open to the possibility. Sharri had
initially been wary for a variety of reasons, mostly related to her
health and her diabetes, but she came around to the idea. She
decided she was open to having another child.

We weren't using birth control, but we weren't determined
to conceive a baby, either. I had been out of town working,
when she was last ovulating, so I didn't expect her to get
pregnant.

Sharri was not overjoyed, to say the least. She was worried.
Sharri was a thirty-eight-year-old type 1 diabetic, and she was
not thrilled at the prospect of going through another pregnancy.
Now she was on her way to the doctor to get confirmation.

I got off the plane and into the airport in Indianapolis, and
even though I was there, I was not there. I was dazed. I didn't
know what to think. Was I sure that *I* wanted this?

I was about to see a few hundred people that I knew at the
Combine. Yet just as I stepped off the plane, just as I began to
make my way to the baggage claim, the first person I ran into
was Kyle Shanahan, who was the offensive coordinator of the
Houston Texans at the time. I had known Kyle since he was
ten years old, because his father, Mike, coached for the Broncos when I was the beat writer there. When he went on to become a wide receiver at Texas, I took him and his best friend
from college, Chris Simms, the son of the CBS analyst Phil
Simms, out to dinner to do a feature on them. Kyle and I always had a good relationship, but now it was about to get very
personal.

Kyle was the very first person I told that my wife was pregnant.

I guess that was fitting since I had known him since he was a little boy. He congratulated me before I grabbed my bags and headed out of the airport, where I bumped into another friend from my Denver days, Rick Smith, then the Houston Texans' general manager. Smith had been the Broncos assistant secondary coach when they won the Super Bowl, and I had gotten to know him over the years as well.

Smith and I decided to share a taxi to downtown Indianapolis, and that gave me a chance to try to process this pregnancy with him. And I said, "I don't understand. She can't be pregnant because she wasn't ovulating at the time."

Rick shook his head and spelled it out to me. "Let me give you a biology lesson. A woman is most likely to get pregnant right before she's ovulating."

I said, "Really? I didn't know that." And I didn't. Which amazed and frightened me. Here I was, a grown man, involved in many relationships before, and I never knew that. They never taught me that in school.

Rick smiled and said, "That's it. Done. Pregnant." What every reporter always seeks: confirmation. And there was more coming.

After I dropped my bags at the downtown Indianapolis Marriott, I called Sharri again. She had taken another test. Another positive.

I asked Rick to meet me for lunch, because by this time, he was married and a father, and I figured he now could give me more than a biology lesson. He could give me a hint of what to expect in the months and years to come. He was in the process of trading quarterback Sage Rosenfels to the Vikings, and I was in the process of a much larger personnel move.

The Combine is a blur, with virtually everybody in the

league talking, gossiping, eating, drinking, negotiating, scouting, and socializing, but it was tough for me to concentrate that night, or the entire week. I went to bed that night after midnight with my head spinning. *Pregnant?* Our team was about to expand its roster.

When Sharri became pregnant in 1999, she had wanted to find out the sex of the child, and Joe did not. Sharri, of course, won. They found out it was a boy and decided to name him Devon, after her grandfather Daniel and her uncle Donald, two men she loved.

She wanted to find out this time, too, and so we did.

We went for the sonogram, and the doctor looked at the monitor and broke the news.

We were having a girl.

A baby girl! This was going to be different for me in every way.

That June, with Sharri around halfway through her pregnancy, I drove to George Maio's golf club, Rockland Country Club, in Sparkill, New York. He was sponsoring a charity golf tournament for the Rockland Country Club Foundation to benefit the Juvenile Diabetes Foundation.

I wasn't sure what to expect, but it would be a strange, memorable day that combined relaxation, intense emotions, and work.

I did not expect the work. It was June, a rare quiet time in the NFL year, but as I drove over the George Washington Bridge, the news broke that New York Giants star Michael

Strahan was retiring. I thought I might have to turn around, go to a local TV studio, and start doing live shots, but I also felt a strong obligation to George. Then I realized that I might be able to honor my obligation to George while making my employer happy. A number of Giants would be attending this golf outing, and I figured I could interview them. So that was how we decided to do it.

When I arrived, I scanned the list of names scheduled to be at the outing: Eli Manning, Tom Coughlin, Tiki Barber, and Jerome Bettis. Those were three prominent Giants and a future Hall of Famer. The NFL Network sent a satellite truck to the club so I could conduct some interviews, which probably sounds a little more intrusive than it actually was. There were celebrities there, and it was a golf outing. It wasn't a solemn affair. It was done for people to be happy and raise money.

I managed to work, play nine holes of golf, and still have lunch with George and meet some of his friends at the club. It was obvious to me that George was beloved there; he knew everyone, and they knew him. He might have been the most popular guy in the room. I wasn't surprised.

But what I remember most about the day was not meeting of any George's friends or interviewing any Giants or NFL people. What I most remember was seeing an engraved stone beneath a flagpole, in memory of Joseph D. Maio:

> *Our friend and fellow member who perished*
> *tragically in the assault on American Liberty of*
> *September 11, 2001. We will never forget!*

For a good five minutes, I stood there staring at it. I got choked up.

Sharri had warmed to the idea of having another child, but she was still scared. Her diabetes meant it would likely be a difficult pregnancy.

Sharri thought her second pregnancy might be as bad as her first. She was wrong.

It was worse.

We found out Sharri was pregnant in February. She was due in October. The months in between were brutal. In early July, she started to have severe stomach pain. Medication didn't help. At 3:30 one morning, she woke up moaning in pain before she fell back asleep.

As I went to the gym that morning, I thought she would be OK. I did not bring my phone into my spinning class, which was a mistake. I should have kept it on me in case Sharri called, but at that point in my life, I never worked out with my phone on me. It was one of those moments when you need to realize you can't do things the way you did as a single guy all those years.

I got out of class and saw I had missed two calls from home. And I knew that meant one thing: trouble. I'd blown it. I called Sharri, and she was as furious at me as she had ever been. When I got home, it wasn't any better.

She ripped into me right there, with Devon watching; I tried to persuade her to wait until he was gone, but she didn't care. I was embarrassed.

"Where the hell were you?" she said.

"I jumped in the shower . . ."

"Are you crazy?! I have to go to the hospital!"

I didn't mean to be insensitive; I just had stuck to my

routine. I had sweat dripping off me, so I jumped in the shower, then rushed right home, but she was so angry. We put Devon on the school bus and drove in silence to her doctor's office. I could feel the fury and fear from her, all the way until we got to the hospital.

By the time we got to her doctor, she was in agony. Something was clearly wrong. I just didn't know what it was. One doctor suspected it was her appendix, and he sent us to the emergency room at North Shore University Hospital.

On our way there, I got a call from a producer at the NFL Network: Brett Favre was asking for his unconditional release from the Green Bay Packers. I said I couldn't help. That was the first time in my two-decade career that I could ever remember saying I was too busy to help and backing away from work, but there was no other option. Nothing mattered more than making sure Sharri was OK.

Sharri needed an MRI, but she was beyond anxious and nervous about taking it. I was worried and felt helpless—I thought the MRI should have been done earlier, and I wasn't convinced that doctors had been giving Sharri the attention she deserved.

Finally, that night, she had an emergency appendectomy. Before she went under, I was told that one in five pregnant women who have their appendixes removed go into premature labor. That was frightening, but we had no options. This was emergency surgery. I tried to digest the possibility. *Sharri could be giving birth this evening. Our daughter could be coming along at any time now.*

The surgery, fortunately, was a success. Sharri did not go into labor. I kept popping into her room in intensive care to check on her, then returning to the waiting room, where a TV was tuned to ESPN and its Brett Favre reporting. Sharri finally left the ICU and got her own room at 2:00 A.M. I saw a chair in there and decided I would sleep in it that night. We'd had a rough morning and a scary evening. I wanted to finish the day by doing the right thing. I wasn't going to leave that hospital until Sharri did.

Our argument about my phone was not an isolated incident. Sharri and I were struggling. I had underestimated the difficulty of walking into her and Devon's life—or perhaps just overestimated my ability to do it. She also had to adjust to having someone else in her life, after years of having to think about only Devon and herself.

Every time I thought I was getting the hang of it, we'd experience some sort of setback. I had connected with Devon when I was dating Sharri, but it was not always so simple once I married her. The issues did not sit well with Sharri, who got mad at me. And she and I were having problems. It was not a good cycle.

A few days after Sharri's appendectomy, I went to the eye doctor. As I sat in the waiting room, I read a stat that 60 percent of second marriages end in divorce. I wrote in my journal:

> *Can't say I knew that, but we could be a statistic at this rate, that's what concerns me.*

That afternoon, I offered to take Devon to GameStop to buy video games. It should have been a simple, fun activity for a kid and his stepdad, but at GameStop, he asked me to buy three games. I told him I thought two was enough, and it was. I came from a background in which I did not get whatever I wanted; limits almost always were imposed. But Sharri liked to indulge Devon. She always wanted him to have the best, because he had experienced the worst.

When I told Devon I would not allow him to get more than two games, he walked out of the store crying. I thought he was acting spoiled, and I didn't care for it. I yelled at him as loudly as I had ever yelled at him. Stepdad or not, it never feels good to yell at a child you love.

We went home. Devon went crying to Sharri, telling her that he wasn't allowed to get what he wanted. I told Sharri my side of the story and marched into my home office, seeking time to calm down, process the situation, and wonder if I could have or should have done anything differently. As I sat alone in my office, Sharri came in to tell me that I had to make Devon dinner, but at that moment, I didn't feel like doing anything for him. That night, Devon went to bed in tears. I was angry and frustrated.

In other words, life happened. I assume that these kinds of days happen in every single family, even the happiest ones, but I felt like they were piling up for us.

I'd talk to friends and compare notes on marital problems. It seemed like everybody had different variations of the same stories, so we were not unusual, but it was still hard.

I had a long history of ending relationships too quickly. I was not about to end this one, but with a baby on the way, I was wondering if I had what it took to make it through and to make the relationship last.

———

Less than a week after Sharri's appendectomy, I was in for a massage appointment when somebody knocked on the door.

"Adam," I was told, "your wife is on the phone. It's an emergency."

Another one. Sharri said she had been struggling to breathe. Well, I wasn't going to screw up this time. I got right up and went home immediately. Sharri's mom met us there. We raced to the hospital and got her into the emergency room.

We were told Sharri might have a pulmonary embolism. Then we were told she had a blood clot in her lung. It sounded disturbing, all of it, whatever it actually was. It turned out to be more disturbing than I even realized. She had a pulmonary embolism and a blood clot in her lung. Sharri, who was already dealing with diabetes, would have to be on blood thinners for a while and deal with twice-a-day injections . . . and of course, she had to be extremely careful in the final months of the pregnancy.

She was discouraged, and understandably so. I sent a group text to some friends, just to vent. *Some people in the summer go to the Hamptons, others go to bed-and-breakfasts, we go to the North Shore Hospital emergency room.*

We kept getting conflicting signals about when Sharri could go home. One doctor said she would soon be released. Then a nurse came in and said she was shocked—*shocked!*—that Sharri was being released. She went on and on about how she never had seen a pregnant woman with a pulmonary embolism be discharged. She talked about the possibility of the blood clot traveling to Sharri's brain.

"You could die," the nurse said.

She went on for fifteen minutes about the dangers of this,

especially for pregnant women, and the damage she had seen it wreak in others. By the end of her medical talk and lesson, Sharri was crying.

I was stuck. Sharri really wanted to get out of there, and I wanted to stick up for her, but what if there was a real danger in having her discharged?

Things that mattered to me before that moment suddenly mattered less, like work. I got emails that Chris Long, the second pick in the NFL Draft, had reached a contract agreement with the St. Louis Rams. This was the kind of story I normally would get to work on right away, but I wrote in my journal:

I couldn't care less, to be honest.

I found myself driving around Long Island, trying to find the right medication for Sharri, physically and mentally exhausted. We had two straight weekends in the hospital, with one incident more unsettling and unnerving than the previous.

Eventually, we got the medication that Sharri needed. Eventually, she got out of the hospital again. And we had to hope that in every way, things would get better.

I suppose most women are ready to be done with their pregnancies by the time they reach full term. Sharri was *really* ready to be done. When we went to see doctors in late September 2008 and they did a sonogram, they found that our soon-to-be-born daughter was weighing in at close to twelve pounds—and Sharri wasn't much over one hundred pounds herself. The sound and reality of it practically made Sharri sick; doctors knew they needed to do the C-section sooner rather than later, lest this baby come out practically a full-grown person. It was a fitting way to end the pregnancy.

Sharri had gone through the pregnancy from hell. And yet, when it came time for the scheduled C-section, she was nervous. So much had already gone wrong, it was fair to wonder what else could. It was hard to feel totally confident about anything anymore. I tossed and turned the night before, so you can imagine what it was like for her.

We left our house at 5:30 A.M. Sharri was quiet, the roads were empty, and it all felt strangely surreal. My mom was very upset that I did not have a Cord Blood Registry kit to save Sharri's blood for the baby in the event of some sort of emergency. We called around to see if we could find one, and we did, at her doctor's office. I was so desperate to get it that I bolted past my father in the lobby without even saying hello to him. He thought it was odd that I was running away from the delivery room and hospital, instead of toward it. But time was of the essence, and I was rushing for everything. I even got pulled over for speeding on the way to the doctor's office. I showed the cop that my wife was about to give birth, and this truly was a life-and-death situation. He responded by staying in his car for ten minutes before finally letting me leave.

I got back to the hospital and immediately changed into scrubs. Then, while I waited to go into Sharri's operating room, I sat in a chair right outside it, contemplating how my life was about to change. This was another one of those moments that always stays with you, forever. I knew my life would change dramatically from the moment I walked in that room to the moment I walked out of it. This was one of those moments we await all our adult years.

I had been parenting Devon for almost two years and really

loved doing it, but this time I would get to be there from the beginning, not miss out on those early years as I had with Devon.

I walked into the room. There was a blue curtain between Sharri and the doctors, and I was on Sharri's side. I tried to get a sense of what was happening that I couldn't see. I thought I heard a cry but didn't. Then I heard them talk about how much hair the baby had. I could see fluid and blood dripping, and the intensity of the moment really hit me.

Then I heard crying, and there she was: our girl.

Dylan Madeline Schefter, named after my beloved grandfather Poppy Dave, whom we had lost to lung cancer in 2002. Dylan weighed eleven pounds, ten ounces—bigger, even, than Devon had been. She was covered in a white film. Sharri joked that she looked like a sausage casing. I was so relieved that the surgery had gone well—the previous few months had been a nightmare, and I had been worried about Sharri. My eyes were watering, the emotions were strong, and then I had this weird thought I had not anticipated. I had spent so much time thinking about Sharri's health.

Now I wondered: Was I supposed to look after Sharri—or Dylan?

The doctors asked me to go back outside for a few minutes while they got Sharri ready for the recovery room. I sat in the same chair I had sat in minutes earlier, but this felt completely different. We had a daughter now. I thought about how many fathers had sat in that same chair and experienced the same powerful emotions I had. That feeling stuck with me for many years.

They wheeled Sharri out, and we saw our families, and I sent an email blast to as many people as I could to share the good news. Of course, everybody was laughing because I was on my BlackBerry. After people started to leave, I gave Sharri a Cartier bracelet that I had bought her. She wasn't expecting it, and she loved it.

All I could really think, though, was that I wanted to see my daughter again. I took my sister, Marni, to the maternity ward to see her, but she wasn't there. It was very odd; this girl had been born minutes earlier, and she wasn't in the maternity ward? I was told she had been moved to intensive care because her sugars were low. Intensive care? Sugars low? We found her, and I couldn't stop looking at her. She was lying under a heat lamp, what looked like a french fry warmer, to take away some of her jaundice and to try to help restore her blood sugars. Her arms flailed out to the sides and were in the shape of goalposts, a position that she would wind up sleeping in for years throughout her childhood—and sometimes even to this day. My happiness was mitigated with concern for her being in intensive care, and our family came by to see our newest addition as well.

Eventually, George Maio was the one who brought Devon to the hospital. Devon came upstairs to the ICU, stared through the glass, and, for the first time, eyed his new baby sister.

After Dylan spent about one week in the hospital in intensive care, we finally were able to bring her home. I quickly realized how much I didn't know. I had never given any thought to baby seats, but we had to have one set up in the back seat of our car. Fortunately, Sharri had parenting experience and knowledge and knew things I didn't. She was the head coach, and I was happy to execute her game plan.

I remember our family pulling up to the house with Dylan, welcoming her to it for the very first time, and thinking as we pulled into the driveway, *This is where you will grow up.* We took her upstairs, into a small room, maybe twelve feet by twelve feet, with yellow painted walls and a white crib, and the changing station that Sharri also knew to have set up in advance.

Now Devon had to adjust yet again to a new person in the house. And again, he did really well. He loved having a little sister. He was well aware that he did not have a conventional family. It was obvious whenever we spoke or wrote our full names.

I was Adam Schefter. Sharri was mainly Sharri Maio, but occasionally Sharri Schefter. Dylan was Dylan Schefter.

But Devon was Devon Maio, not Schefter. He never wanted to become Devon Schefter. We never wanted him to lose his connection to *Maio*, not Joe, nor Joe's family, nor the name with which he entered the world. To his credit, Devon said, "I don't want to disrespect my grandparents. I want to keep my last name." It was a really mature thought.

And Sharri wanted the same last name as her son, so she largely remained Sharri Maio.

So there we were: two Schefters, two Maios, one family. Devon knew this was unusual, but he also always knew he was loved. He received a lot more affection than many people who come from traditional two-parent homes. And his extended family was large and loving, too.

He was still so close to all six of his grandparents. He had Sharri's family, my family, and the Maio family, who always treated Devon like a prince. He had a lot of older cousins on that side, and they doted on him. His appearances were like an event: "Devon's coming!"

Devon always especially loved Joe's brother, his uncle Anthony. I would watch them play together and almost be jealous of their connection. Anthony was the epitome of the fun uncle you read about. I understood why Devon felt the way he did. I enjoyed Anthony's company, too. We were not in constant contact—he lived his life, with his wife and three daughters, and we lived ours—but family is family.

When Devon was young, I used to joke with Sharri that he liked Uncle Anthony more than he liked me. I was teasing, but it did feel that way sometimes. Anthony and Devon had a special bond. Some adults struggle to connect with kids. Anthony did it naturally. One year, he built Devon a trampoline for his birthday. Devon always adored him.

14

When I was forty-three, I was dealing with a potentially disconcerting medical issue. I had a lump on my neck and two red splotches on my back. I didn't know what the lump meant, but lumps worry everybody. I made a doctor's appointment to see how concerned I should be.

On the morning of the appointment, I went to the gym to work out first. When I got out and went to my locker and grabbed my BlackBerry, I saw a text from my friend Jon Miller, who works at NBC but belonged to the same golf club as the Maios.

Is the story true about Anthony Maio? he texted.

And I thought, *Was* what *story true about Anthony Maio?* I knew Jon had a friendship with Anthony, but I had no idea what he was talking about.

I responded, *What's the story—first I've heard of anything.*

Jon wrote, *Heard some sad news about Anthony Maio but don't know if it's true—lots of rumors. Car accident?*

I was not expecting that. I had heard nothing. I told him I would do what I always do when I want information: I would make some calls. But before I could dial the first number of the first person I would have called, Sharri called me.

"You're not going to believe this," she said.

I knew she had to be calling for the same reason Jon had texted.

I said, "Anthony Maio."

She was surprised to hear me say that. "How'd you know?" she asked.

I didn't think that was important at the moment. I didn't need to explain the text from Jon Miller.

"What happened?" I asked.

And she said, "He died—"

"*Died!?*"

I was stunned. Actually, *stunned* doesn't cover it. It came out of nowhere for me. This was one of those moments in life where you just know immediately that everything has changed, irrevocably. I tried to fully grasp just how devastating this was.

Anthony was gone.

His three daughters, Nicolette, Dominique, and Julianna, had lost their daddy.

His wife, Carmela, was suddenly a widow.

Devon had lost an uncle he loved so much and a close link to the daddy he didn't remember.

I understood right away that for Sharri, a wound that had mostly healed had been ripped open again. She would have to go back to the cemetery where Joe was buried to see Anthony buried next to him. This would bring her back to that emotional place she had worked so hard to escape.

And for Paula and George . . . well, that's what actually

concerned me most. What could I even say? They had lived through every parent's worst nightmare—with grace and dignity, no less. They didn't become bitter, angry people after Joe died. They warmly welcomed me and then Dylan into their family. And now here they were, forced to live through this nightmare again. After burying one son, they now were going to be forced to bury their other.

Sharri called Little Joe to see if he knew anything. He didn't know a lot of details, they still were coming in, but he did know this:

Anthony had taken his own life.

Our first reactions are not always the ones that make us proudest or that others say we are supposed to have, but I will be honest here. My first reaction, when I found out that Anthony took his own life, was to be mad.

I wondered: How could he do this to his parents? How could he do it to his kids? I had seen firsthand what Joe's death had done to Paula and George. As much as I loved being in Devon's life, my heart always hurt for him, because I knew he would never have the kind of relationship with his real father that he deserved. Anthony had been one of Devon's favorite people. I was mad that Anthony would force Devon to cope with his death.

I did not know how Anthony could do this to so many people he loved. I was so sad to hear the news, but I was also angry at what struck me, at the time, as a selfish act. Didn't he realize how much devastation this would cause?

The news came so quickly that I didn't even know what to do. It wasn't like he became deathly ill and we could visit him in the hospital. It took us minutes to find out he was gone. I went home and saw Sharri, who was crying as she talked on the phone with her mom.

My head was in a fog. I kept my appointment with my doctor, who diagnosed me with shingles. That seemed insignificant now. I braced for the moment when Devon got off the school bus and we would give him the news. I was in a daze that afternoon as I rushed to get back home to be there for Devon when he got home from school.

In the parking lot of my doctor's office, I backed into a concrete pole.

I drove home and watched Devon get off the bus. He thought it was just another school day: go home, get something to eat. But we knew better. As he stepped off the bus, I was thinking, *This is a day that he will remember for the rest of his life.*

Sharri stepped to the bus to help him off the steps. Once he got down, she pulled him aside.

"Dev, I've got some sad news," she said. "Anthony died."

He was confused.

"Anthony who?" he asked.

"Your uncle Anthony," she said.

He said, "Seriously?"

That was his reaction: *Seriously?* He said it as if we were telling him we wanted him to skip homework to watch a movie instead. He said it very calmly, very matter-of-factly, without any emotion at that time. Devon was a month away from turning ten years old. He couldn't quite grasp how his uncle could suddenly be gone. There had been no indication this was coming. Anthony had not been sick. It didn't seem real to Devon.

But then we went in the house and it hit him. He went upstairs and started bawling.

We left Dylan with my mother and drove to the Maio house in New Jersey. The sky was gray, the air misty. This was the drive Sharri had been too scared to make in the months after 9/11. It was extremely difficult to comprehend the reason we were making it now: Anthony had committed suicide in Florida.

We arrived at the Maios' and walked inside. When George saw Sharri and Devon, George started wailing. That was the only word that came to mind: *wailing*. You could know somebody for fifty years and never see them cry like that.

George's mother was crying and calling out to God: "Why didn't He take me?"

Sharri walked out to the deck to see Carmela and hug her. I looked out at them, these two women in the prime of their lives, and thought, *Wow. These are the two women who lost the Maio boys*. It was a powerful image and an unimaginable reality.

I tried talking to George, delicately asking what had happened. He told me he had gotten the news the night before, when a Florida police officer called and asked if he was home. George said he wasn't. The officer told George to call when he got home. George told me he knew right then that Anthony had died.

In the house, I found none of the anger that I initially felt when I first heard the news. Everybody was just crushed. Paula was questioning the existence of God. After three hours, we turned to head home, but there was no way to detach ourselves from the scene. Even when I stopped for gas, Devon started crying because he remembered being at that gas station with Uncle Anthony. That night, I woke at 4:00 A.M. with a headache, and I just lay there in bed, thinking about Anthony being gone. It didn't seem real.

The next morning, when Dylan got up, I walked into her room to get her. She was nineteen months old, far too young to understand what was happening to her family. I started to really understand what it must have been like when Joe died. Back then, Devon was almost fifteen months old, far too young to understand what was happening to his family.

I looked at Dylan.

"Adam," she said. This was what Devon always called me, and she was imitating her big brother.

"No," I corrected her. "Daddy."

She started crying. I guess she really wanted to call me Adam, just like Devon. It was one of those funny, unexpected moments you have as a parent, and it was completely incongruous with what was happening to our family. That day, I took Dylan to a nearby duck pond, where she fed the ducks and saw a turtle and remained blissfully oblivious to what was going on in our world and the Maios' world.

Sharri and I wanted to make things better for Paula and George, but we knew that was impossible. Their boys were gone. What could we, or anyone, even say? We tried to help in the smallest ways, because that was all we could do. We picked up paper goods, enough paper goods to last a year, to take to their house, and drove there to try to provide whatever comfort we could.

Friends who gathered in those days at the Maios' house would wonder: If Joe had lived, would Anthony have lived, too? The brothers were so close. Anthony never fully recovered from Joe's death.

There is no way to know how much Joe's death contributed

to the end of Anthony's life. Sometimes there just are no answers, only questions, and this one always will linger.

But we also started to hear about the inner turmoil that might have led Anthony to take his own life. People who had spoken to Anthony in the previous few months could tell he wasn't right. He said things that didn't make sense. He made purchases that defied logic. A few people were worried about his mental state. We didn't know any of this until after he died.

He had been taking a drug called Chantix to stop smoking. There had been reports of thousands of mental-health issues linked to Chantix use, including suicidal thoughts. The drug had been hit with a so-called black-box label warning that it could cause life-threatening conditions. Pfizer, which settled numerous lawsuits related to the drug, fought the black-box warning and, with the benefit of new clinical trial data, convinced regulators to remove it in 2016. Still, we couldn't help but wonder whether Chantix contributed to Anthony's suicide.

On the day Anthony died, a friend went to pick him up for dinner. The shower was running. The friend called for Anthony to get ready. When there was no response for five minutes, the friend went to check on Anthony. He found Anthony slumped down, as if his feet had slipped out from under him. The friend told me that for days after that, every time he closed his eyes, he saw Anthony on the floor. Paramedics said Anthony was gone in ten seconds. They found a note next to him.

I looked around the house, at Dylan and Devon and Sharri, and other people in the Maio family. There were pictures of Anthony and Joe all over the house. It was hard to look away.

———

The wake, at the Pizzi Funeral Home in Northvale, New Jersey, did not bring peace or closure. Honestly, it just brought more misery, but it also brought signs of great character. On the first day of the wake, George stood right next to the open casket, hovering above his fallen son, greeting every guest, with pictures of Anthony all around. I turned to Sharri and told her how blown away I was by George's strength. How he stood next to his son, with images of his son all around, and maintained his composure was a test of manhood many could not pass.

The next day, we went back and watched George do it all again. It was incredible. I don't know how he did it.

Even with mourners walking past Anthony's open casket to pay their respects, Devon said he wouldn't look at his uncle, but at times, I caught him taking a peek; it was as if he couldn't resist getting another look at the uncle he'd loved and lost. At other times that week, Devon seemed happy to be around the Maio family, who have always treated him so well. There were far too many emotions for a not-yet-ten-year-old to fully process.

Throughout the wake, my eyes kept drifting toward a picture to the right of the casket. The picture was of Joe and Anthony, together, each kissing Paula's cheek at Anthony's wedding. Paula wore a smile that looked like it would last forever. The family looked so happy, so together, so alive. Now two of the three people in the picture were gone. Every time I looked at the picture, I cried.

The funeral was just as heartbreaking. Nicolette and Dominique spoke beautifully about their father, how much he meant to them, and how much they would miss him. It was hard to listen to Anthony's daughters eulogize him and not cry. As the pallbearers carried Anthony's coffin, Paula threw herself on it, wailing out loud. It was hard to watch.

Afterward, we walked to the grave site and placed roses on Anthony's tombstone. It was right next to Joe's: side by side, brother to brother.

Sharri had not gone to the cemetery since Joe had died. Sometimes Sharri wondered if people judged her for not visiting the burial site, but she thought about Joe every day. That was how she paid tribute to him. There were reminders of his life everywhere, in her mind and in her home. She did not need to be that close to a reminder of his death.

Now she had to go. I wondered if she might break down, but she managed to keep it together—another Maio showing extraordinary strength. The moment that she would remember from that day was when Devon saw his great-grandmother, Nanna Bubs, crying. She was George's mother.

When Anthony's son had died, and he told everybody the boy's name was Anthony Joseph, Nanna Bubs said she had a hard time seeing the names Anthony and Joseph on a tombstone. It reminded her so much of Anthony and Joe.

Now Anthony and Joe were both gone. It was more than Nanna Bubs could take.

Without anybody prompting him, Devon walked over to her, sat down next to her, and put his arm around her to comfort her. He was only nine years old, but he knew exactly how to comfort somebody, and he wasn't afraid to do it. Sharri watched him and she thought about Joe sleeping on the floor next to their sick dog, and she thought, *Wow. He is just like Joe.*

15

In the summer of 2013, right before Dylan started prekindergarten, her school held back-to-school night. Parents were invited in to see the school and meet the teachers. Hanging on the wall in Dylan's classroom were the students' names and their birthdays. Sharri and I noticed another girl, Maelyn, was born on Dylan's birthday, October 3.

We went through the night's introductory activities, which lasted around an hour, and on the way out, I happened to start chatting with another father named Charlie Burgdorf. He said he had four kids from his first marriage, then got divorced, met a woman, and remarried. He and his second wife had a daughter named Maelyn.

I said, "Oh, the October 3 Maelyn?"

He said, "Yeah."

I explained that our daughter was the October 3 Dylan.

We kept talking. Charlie said his wife, Christina, had been married but was widowed.

"I'm very sorry to hear that," I said. "Do you mind me asking what happened?"

He said, "She lost her husband on 9/11."

Everybody has a story, and theirs was uncannily similar to ours. Dylan and Maelyn were delivered in the same hospital, hours apart, by the same doctor. Christina's deceased husband, Richard, was the son of former New York Giants linebacker and broadcaster Dick Lynch. Christina and Richard had a daughter, Olivia, who was born three days before Devon, but also was due on the day Devon was born, June 21. Christina went to a Catholic girls' high school in Syosset, New York; Sharri went to Syosset High School, in the same town. Christina went to Northeastern University; Sharri spent a year at Northeastern University.

The similarities felt eerie to us, in the same way that me having the same birthday as Joe felt eerie.

Dylan wasn't thinking about all this when she met Maelyn. They were both too young to be conscious of how other people would tell their life stories. Dylan was aware that Devon had a father before I came along, but she didn't think about it too much. And yet, Maelyn and Dylan formed an instant bond. They have been close friends since they met. They are similar in temperament and disposition. They often seem like sisters— as though they were meant to be together from the day they were born.

The similarities between Maelyn and Dylan reinforced to us that the circumstances of our lives are not unique. There are times when you can feel alone, but that doesn't mean you are.

It was also a reminder of what Sharri had learned over time and says often: *Everybody has something.*

A death of a loved one, a disease, a divorce, an addiction, a horrible relationship with a family member—everybody has something painful and personal they must deal with. Nobody goes through life unscathed. My grandfather Poppy Dave, whom Dylan was named after, would put it like this: "Nobody gets a free ride."

Sharri lived an extremely fortunate life until Joe was killed. The attacks on 9/11 had rendered her a stay-at-home mother in a new house with no husband. She was lonely, and she felt bad for herself. When she went shopping, she would see other mothers and fathers together with their kids and think, *I wish I were in their place. I would give anything to be them.*

Months passed. Then years. She talked to her friends, listened to their problems, and thought, *I'm not sure I want to be in that position either.* She realized that life is challenging for everybody. Her grief never fully dissipated, but the self-pity did.

When you have experienced the worst of humanity, you can be defeated or you can look for the best of humanity. We have seen the best of it. I have seen it in Paula and George, in Sharri and Devon, and even in Joe. His impact is still evident.

Even in death, Joe continues to prod people to do what they should do but don't really want to do, to live their lives the way he lived his. Kim Rothofsky, Joe's friend from childhood, says she still thinks of him almost every day, even though they had fallen out of touch a few years before Joe died.

Duane Tarrant, another friend from childhood, says Joe's death made him take a hard look at his relationship with his girlfriend, Joanne Mucerino. They had broken up a few times.

Joanne worked on the twenty-third floor of one of the towers. She got out. Duane thought about Sharri and thought, *That could be me*. He and Joanne got married and have two kids together.

Jordan Bergstein had been in a funk in the summer of 2001—his degenerative eye condition, retinitis pigmentosa, was starting to profoundly change his life, and it caused a lot of emotional pain. After Joe died, and the initial shock and devastation wore off, Jordan's outlook changed completely. He shed his despair, even as his vision kept getting worse. Jordan thought about his friend Joe, with his endless passion for life, and realized that as limited as his own vision was, he still got to see more in his life than Joe did.

"Joe's death," he says, "has helped me live."

And when Adam Gordon was in his late thirties . . . after Joe Maio had helped him lose his virginity . . . after Adam had brought a number of women back to their Upper East Side apartment and been intimate with them . . . after Adam had married one of Sharri's best friends . . . after Adam and his wife had three children . . . and long after Joe had been killed, Adam started to realize:

I'm gay.

He came out of the closet when he was forty, but his life did not immediately turn into a *Will and Grace* episode. He had some hard times. He lost his job, moved to California, and could barely pay child support. And he thought, *If Joey were here, this wouldn't happen*. Joe would have protected him. He believed that with every beat of his heart.

Eventually he started doing better. He was happy. And he kept thinking, *I wish Joe could see me now*. And so, once a year,

Adam Gordon writes a letter to Joe, to let him know how he is doing.

You hear people talk about moving on. There is no moving on. Moving on means forgetting, and who wants to forget?

Sharri's life with me did not replace her life with Joe. The two lives are now joined together. When she was married to Joe, her favorite day of the week was Sunday. Those were family days. On Saturdays, Joe would often play golf for half the day, but they spent Sundays together. So after he died, Sundays were the hardest for her.

Now, because I cover the NFL, I often work on Sundays. It's the big day of the NFL week. Sharri has a tough time with it; so all these years later, Sundays still are hardest for her. When I'm in Bristol, working each Sunday, Sharri misses both of her husbands.

We have a pretty easy day-to-day relationship. I try not to ask for too much. I want to be able to do my job and get my morning workouts in, and sometimes I'll suggest what we should eat for dinner. That is pretty much it.

We have a really strong marriage. I can see now that my concerns years ago were largely a product of my own expectations. I have learned that part of being in a successful relationship is understanding it will not be perfect. We have our little disagreements. She will be arguing with Dylan in the bathroom while I'm ignoring them so I can set my NBA fantasy lineup, which of course drives her crazy. *Don't you hear me yelling in the bathroom?!*

And she will tell you that I am useless when it comes to

everyday household problems. She'll say I have no idea where the circuit breaker box is. One time recently, the toilet wouldn't flush, so she had to reach in the tank and fix the chain. She thought, *If this were Adam, he would be peeing in the woods.* Like many women who are married to men, Sharri doesn't really understand how I was able to survive on my own. I try to explain: I worked, I brought my laundry to a Laundromat that charged me seventy-five cents per pound, and I ordered takeout. It was not that complicated.

I try to be the best son-in-law I can be for Paula and George, even though I am technically not their son-in-law. Sometimes George will text Sharri, and she won't get back to him right away. That's just her style. She doesn't treat phone calls and text messages with the same urgency that some people do. But George gets nervous. He worries. So he'll text me, and I tell him, right away, moments after his text: *Pop, everything's OK.*

We don't talk a lot about Joe and Anthony, but I think about what happened to Paula and George all the time. Two sons, both gone. No time to prepare for either. No chance to say goodbye.

I am continually amazed that Paula and George have treated me like a son-in-law. I try to treat them with the same respect and affection that I offer Sharri's parents. I look around, and there are people who won't talk to their in-laws at all. We've all heard "my mother-in-law" jokes. There is a reason for that. A lot of people can't stand to be in the same room as their in-laws. I have a great relationship with the Maios, even though it's unconventional, and I love Sharri's parents like I love my own.

I have two great sets of in-laws. Sharri has two sets of in-laws. Our kids have three sets of grandparents. It's kind of like a weird permutation, like a child with six toes. It's not bad or a lesser version of what you normally see. It's just different.

Paula and George never resented my presence. They embraced it. They never acted like Sharri was forgetting or disrespecting Joe by being with me. A lot of people in their situation would have acted that way. I'm very fortunate.

I am also very conscious of the fact that the deaths of Joe and Anthony are an enormous cloud over Paula and George. They live with a lot of pain. It never subsides. When you pour your hearts into raising two boys, and they are your life, and they both die in inexplicable tragedies, what do you do?

Paula and George don't talk about the pain all the time, but I know it's there. It has to be. They are in a different emotional place from where even Sharri is, because losing a child is different from losing a spouse, and they lost both of theirs. Sharri has built a second adult life for herself, with a second husband and two children. It's an opportunity she was granted. That's a lot harder to do when you are older and you have lost your children. Still, Paula and George are an essential presence in our lives, and they handle each day with grace and dignity.

I have great, great respect and love for them.

And I have tried my best to help raise their grandson.

16

The little boy that Joe Maio left behind became a schoolboy and then a teenager. Anthony's words, spoken at Joe's funeral, were heartbreaking at the time. They became even more chilling after Anthony died. But Devon is an incredibly resilient kid. If there is a hole in his heart, he hides it well.

Devon rarely asks about Joe. I don't know if people would consider that normal or not. It's just the way he is. If you have spoken to people who were adopted—or if you were adopted yourself—then you know that some adoptees long to meet their birth parents, and others have very little interest. This is obviously a very different situation, but it helps explain Devon's mind-set. He has no memories of his father. He lives what we think is a great life with Sharri, me, Dylan, and our dogs. I know he thinks about Joe, but I don't think he spends as much of his time wondering about Joe as strangers might imagine. One day I think he will; it might mean even more to him as he gets older and becomes a father of his own. But now, it does not seem to weigh down his days.

Sharri is different. She thinks about Joe every day, but especially at the milestone moments in Devon's life. What would Joe think of his boy entering high school? Would Joe be the one who could get Devon cranking on his college essays?

She wonders: What would be different if Joe were alive? What would their relationship be like? Would they have a strong bond? Nobody knew Devon and Joe as well as Sharri does.

She thinks Joe would understand Devon in ways that I don't. It's easy to picture Joe telling Devon how to talk to a customer, or to envision Devon copying his father's golf swing—then using it to outdrive his old man.

When she fights with Devon, she thinks, *How would Joe handle this situation?* Then she realizes that thinking about it will get her nowhere, so she tries to block it out of her mind.

Sharri looks at Devon and sees Joe. His face. His smile. His attitude.

George looks at Devon and sees Joe. His skin. His teeth. His mannerisms. Devon had a growth spurt at the same age that his father did. He carries himself just like Joe.

Devon has an easy confidence about him, just like Joe did. Like a lot of teenage boys, he is not the most orderly kid. He does well in school, but not always as well as he could. He knows when he can coast, and he does. Joe would understand. When Joe went to Boston University, he did not always work that hard. He did not get the best grades. He would go out on a Wednesday night, leaving his roommate Cory Tovin with books spread out on the dinner table, and then he would come home at midnight and say, incredulously, "You've been sitting here for *five hours*?"

Cory would explain that he was studying. It was what college students did. Joe didn't do it that much. But Cory always knew Joe would be successful.

Sometimes Devon is so relaxed that it drives me crazy. I want him to push, to hustle, to go hard after what he wants instead of just making his way toward it. Sometimes I ask Sharri why he doesn't do that, and she laughs and says, "Because he's not you." She is absolutely right. Devon is going to be very successful doing things his way, and he will be happy.

And maybe one day he'll tell me that he has it right, that I have it wrong, and I need to be more like him and let up and live a bit.

I'm not wired like Devon and Joe. I'm a grinder. I always have been because I've never felt as if I had any obvious talents, so I had to work to make up for it. When I was a freshman at the University of Michigan, I tried to rush a fraternity but didn't get in, so I went to the football office to see if they needed somebody to pick up jock straps and hand out water bottles. They didn't need anybody. So I went to the basketball office to see if they needed somebody to pick up jock straps and hand out water bottles. They didn't need anybody.

I just wanted to be part of something and work as hard as I could. It's how I ended up at the school newspaper, *The Michigan Daily*. Nobody else would have me; *The Michigan Daily* turned away nobody. Any professional success I've had I attribute to my work ethic, not talent. I have had my foot on the gas pedal since college, trying to do all the right things. I try to return every text message and call everybody back and be as reliable for my employer as I am for one of my colleagues.

Success in my job is predicated on constant communication. *Constant.* I am in the information business. The more information I have, the more information I get. When people in the NFL talk about what's happening in the league—who might get drafted where, which coaches are in trouble, who just got hurt in practice—you're either part of that conversation or not. I need to be part of that conversation. There is no other option. So my phone is like one of my appendages.

Sharri is not like that. She doesn't check her email fifty times a day. She doesn't drop everything when a text comes in; sometimes it will be hours, or days, before she even notices the text. I'll ask her, "Did you see my text? Did you get that email?" and she will say, "No. I'm not on my phone like you. I'm not married to it."

In some ways, we are very different. Sharri is laid-back; I'm not. I want things done yesterday. I want them to be done right and as soon as possible. When we send out our holiday cards every year, they always go out the week of Thanksgiving, long before the holiday rush. I always want our cards to be the first in the mailbox, before the wave of cards from everybody else. Sharri laughs at me. "What happens if somebody else's card gets there the day before?" But that's just me. I want to get things done *now*.

That is why my job suits my personality. Or maybe my personality has been molded by my job.

My career started to grow a year after Dylan was born. My original five-year deal with the NFL Network was expiring, and we were unable to agree on a new deal. I just wasn't comfortable with the offer. One Friday in March, after the network told me it was a take-it-or-leave offer, I told people at the network I had to leave it; it wasn't fair.

My contract was not up for another six months, but they pulled me off the air immediately. The following Monday, the contents of my office arrived at my house, packed up in two boxes. Someone at the league office had cleaned out my office for me.

So I negotiated a deal with ESPN instead. And after it was finalized, I asked the NFL Network to let me out of my deal early—this way, the network wouldn't have to pay me for six months to do nothing, and I could start at ESPN right away. The people who ran the network declined. They decided they would rather pay me to do nothing than not pay me and have me work at a competitor.

It was silly, but as I have learned throughout my life, things don't always happen the way you want them to happen. What matters is how you handle it. I didn't want to leave the NFL Network; I made so many friends there who I remain friendly with to this day. There were some great people in my life.

The funny thing is, when I accepted the job at ESPN, I didn't even know what I would be doing for the network. I knew they were hiring me for news and information and also because they were about to launch a new 9:00 A.M. *SportsCenter*, but I later found out that they planned to include me on their *Sunday NFL Countdown* show, with broadcasting legends Chris Berman, Tom Jackson, and Chris Mortensen. I had no idea my job would include that when I accepted the offer, and I laugh when I think about it today. Who takes a job without knowing exactly what it entails? I did. Glass half-full. Blind faith. Me.

Moving to ESPN turned out to be one of the best things that happened to me. I joined Twitter around the same time, which gave me an outlet for breaking news. At ESPN, I achieved more than I ever could have imagined possible when I started covering the Broncos or even when I joined the NFL Network, and now I had some balance in my life. I had people who were more important to me than my work.

Craig Esposito still says I changed after I met Sharri. Devon changed me as well. And then Dylan changed me again. Craig would know. He saw me at my lowest point. He saw the void, and then he saw how my family filled it.

Of course, there were times I reverted back, and work took hold. I tried to balance work life and family life.

I would get to do live shots for ESPN from my home office most days, which allowed me to take Dylan out to lunch every day. Each day, I would get done with a TV hit, and we would head out to a local eating establishment for soup or a sandwich and some daddy-daughter time. But one day in 2012, as I filled up the car with gas after eating lunch, with Dylan asleep in her car seat, I got a text that the St. Louis Rams were wrapping up the search for the most coveted head coaching candidate that year and hiring Jeff Fisher. I rushed to file the story to the ESPN news desk from my phone and to post it on Twitter. And right after I did, one of the *SportsCenter* producers called to ask how quickly I could get home to be on *SportsCenter*. I told them, "Minutes."

I paid for the gas and rushed home as quickly as I could. All I could think about was the ramifications of the Rams hiring Fisher and the impact it had on other teams, like the Miami Dolphins, who also were looking for a head coach. I raced into my driveway, ran into the house, got wired up for the live shot as quickly as I could, and popped on air to deliver the news: Jeff Fisher to St. Louis.

Sharri popped her head into my office and calmly asked, "Where's Dylan?"

And then it hit me. In my haste to get on air as soon as possible, I had accidentally left Dylan asleep in the car. It was only for a few minutes. But it was a reminder that working can never override parenting.

17

I have tried to do everything I can to give Devon a great childhood like I had and like Joe had. Because of my job, I have been able to give him some unbelievable sporting experiences that a lot of adults would call "bucket list" items. We sat behind the Mets dugout for a World Series game against the Royals—and nearly got taken out by a screaming line drive that someone hit right at us. We watched North Carolina's basketball team play Duke in Cameron Indoor Stadium. We went to a Michigan game in Michigan Stadium and stood on Michigan's sideline. We watched Dirk Nowitzki pass Shaquille O'Neal for number six on the NBA's all-time scoring list in Brooklyn, and afterward, Nowitzki gave Devon his jersey. We even went to Green Bay one December day to shoot a Gillette razor commercial with three Packers offensive linemen—David Bakhtiari, Corey Linsley, and Don Barclay—with Devon spending time talking to them about playing offensive line, the position he played in high school.

During some Junes, I've taken part in this Best Buddies football event that Tom Brady hosts in Massachusetts. I've participated a few years. I play on a team. Devon comes along and is right there with all the Patriots and celebrities in attendance, though he still most remembers eating multiple lobsters at the function's clambake one year.

In 2018, I took Devon and two of his high school buddies to their first-ever Super Bowl, letting them experience some of what I had for the past twenty-five years.

There are kids who would be so excited to be there that they would start shaking. Not Devon. I think Devon thinks this is all cool—but not as cool as I would have thought when I was his age. I was a sports-obsessed kid. Devon just isn't like that. He's a quiet kid. He isn't into the show. He isn't one of those kids who dreams of meeting his sports idols. They're just people to him. He doesn't play fantasy football, doesn't care much about it, and barely watches the NFL when it's on TV. He did play high school football—with the rule that if he suffered one concussion, he would be done playing. He made it to the end of his senior year without getting a concussion.

He went about his job on the football field in a tough, quiet way—never showboating, never celebrating, just quietly going about his business.

He is, in other words, a lot like his father.

Joe loved sports but did not spend hours at a time watching them, and he certainly didn't obsess over them. People in the New York area have so many local teams that even being loyal to your hometown means making a choice: Giants or Jets; Yankees or Mets; Knicks or Nets; Rangers, Islanders, or Devils. If you ask one of Joe's friends today to name Joe's favorite teams, they might be stuck. His identity was not tied to being a fan.

Despite our personality differences, Devon and I have a very good relationship. I've tried to teach him not so much by words but by example. He can watch the hours and time I put in, the commitment that a job can take, the effort it commands, and hopefully one day that will stay with him when he's in the working world. Most of all, he knows I love him, and I know he loves me.

Devon is still too young to really have a full perspective on his family—he needs to move out, be out in the world, and see how other families are. It's hard to see what your family life was like when you are still in the middle of it. But Sharri thinks in a few years, he will be thankful that he had me in his life. I hope she's right.

Devon does not call me *Dad*. He calls me *Ad*, short for *Adam*; it's like I'm missing a *D*. To me, he is my son. It's how I introduce him to people, and how I think of him. But once in a while, he will say something about "my dad," meaning Joe, and it stops me. I am reminded then that, while I seem like his dad and feel like his dad and do everything I can to be his dad, I'm not actually his dad. I think Devon sees me as a father figure, but there is a difference between a father figure and a father. Joe was Devon's father. He still is.

The dynamics with Dylan are different. There are a few reasons for that: me being there from the moment she was born; me having some experience raising Devon before Dylan came along; her being a girl; and the fact that her personality is very different from Devon's. Dylan is talkative, loud, outgoing, and out-front. Devon prefers remaining in the background.

But we have all come to accept that those differences are

OK. You don't have to have the exact same relationship with each of your kids. That's not natural. What matters is having a great relationship with each of them in their own way, and I believe I do. I don't think Devon views me as the guy who married his mom. We're beyond that. I'm part of his family, I'm the dad he knows, and we love each other.

Devon and Sharri share a sarcastic sense of humor. Sometimes they laugh at me because they think I don't get it. Meanwhile, I'm so consumed by whatever I have to do next that sometimes I miss things.

Dylan has a sarcastic side, too, but she is more of an extrovert than Devon and more intense—like me. As I mentioned earlier, I never missed a day of school growing up. Not one. Sharri thinks that's crazy. She asks me, "Didn't you ever get sick? You never threw up?" I took pride in being there every day. I'm still proud of it. Dylan knows I never missed a day of school, and she is determined to match me. She is competitive like that.

Dylan has always had an active imagination and natural charisma. She is such an extrovert that sometimes Sharri thinks, *Is this actually my child?* When we visit Dylan's school, it's pretty clear that everybody there knows her. She's saying hello to older kids, younger kids, every kid.

Dylan seems like she was born for show business. I'm sure my job makes it seem normal to her, but she is just drawn to the stage. In the summer of 2017, she was ESPN's kid correspondent on the red carpet at the ESPY Awards; she interviewed Steph Curry, Joel Embiid, Odell Beckham Jr., and others. It went so well that, a month later, ESPN assigned her to do more interviews after a Patriots-Lions preseason game in Detroit.

There are some veteran reporters who are intimidated by New England Patriots coach Bill Belichick. But there was Dylan, sticking a microphone in his face and saying, "You're known for rocking sweatshirts. What's your wardrobe this season?"

She arm-wrestled the Patriots' Rob Gronkowski. ("I don't think you're even trying," she told him.) She asked Tom Brady, "Who wears the football pants in your family, you or Giselle?"

Brady asked her where she would go to college, and she said, "Probably where my dad went: Michigan." Brady said, "I went there, too!" and gave her a high five.

She told Belichick that I'm no help around the house and can't screw in a light bulb. (I wonder where she got that idea!) Belichick said, "I bet your dad's better than you think he is. I bet he can do a lot of stuff around the house." Dylan shook her head with perfect comic timing and said, "I don't think so." Who thinks on their feet that fast, especially while talking to an NFL coaching legend?

She asked several players, "What advice do you have for an eight-year-old?" I think Lions quarterback Matthew Stafford probably had the best answer:

"You seem like you've got it all figured out at the moment, so I don't know. Maybe I should be taking advice from you."

A lot of kids might *say* they want to do red carpet interviews or talk to famous athletes, but then they would get a microphone in their hands and freeze. Not Dylan. She was completely in her element. I don't think she fully understands that these people are celebrities or a lot of people might be watching. She just loves it. We did some interviews with NFL players and were supposed to go to Dallas for the Cowboys-Raiders game, but we had to cut off the Texas portion of the trip because

Hurricane Harvey was coming, and she was actually very up-set. She didn't want to miss a thing and wanted to complete the job.

She was so good that we brought her in the studio, where she talked about the experience. She called Brady "the most generous, kind person that I met—and you can't fake that."

Did she like interviewing people?

"I love it," Dylan said on *NFL Live*. "I get to work with my dad."

18

As Dylan grew up, we told her bits and pieces about Joe. She knew her mom was married to Joe before she married me. She knew Joe was Devon's father. She knew he was beloved. But for a long time, she didn't know too much more than that. It's just not a story you can share with a little kid.

In the summer of 2016, she started to learn. The fifteen-year anniversary of the 9/11 attacks fell on an NFL Sunday, so ESPN asked if it could do a video story about our family's connection to that date. We shot some of it in our backyard over the course of a few days. I wrote and narrated the piece, while the great ESPN producer Dominique Collins put it together.

I remember sitting on the *SportsCenter* set the Thursday before the piece ran for the first time on *Sunday NFL Countdown*. I received a text from the head of ESPN's NFL features department, Greg Jewell, who initially pushed the idea of this story through. He had just seen the piece, and he texted me: *Leaving edit . . . Cried several times . . . One thing to realize:*

your kids will watch this when they are 50 and cry . . . your grandkids will watch this . . . This piece will live forever.

Even my NFL boss, Seth Markman, the man primarily responsible for bringing me to ESPN, texted: *This piece . . . Wow. Unreal.*

I was anxious to see what they were talking about, but more for Sharri and the Maios than for myself. I wanted the piece to honor Joe and his memory in the most dignified way. I wanted to make sure the piece was more about him than about me.

On that Friday night, September 9, Sharri finally agreed to sit down to watch it. It took her time to build up to be ready; it was not something she was looking forward to. In the hallway of our home, in almost the exact spot where I proposed to her, we sat on the floor and watched it. She sat silently. It was hard to know exactly what she was thinking or feeling, but fortunately, she liked it and approved of it.

It just so happened that Dylan happened to have a playdate that night at our house with Maelyn.

Dylan is an exuberant kid; when she heard that we were watching the story that the ESPN crew had been filming at our house earlier that summer, she grabbed Maelyn, all excited, and invited her to come watch her and our family on TV. We were thinking, *Dylan, this isn't the type of thing you get excited about.* But she was seven years old. She wasn't capable of processing these things like an adult would. She had heard a lot about Joe, but he was still an idea to her as much as a real person. She didn't really understand how he had died. In fact, Dylan never had been told about 9/11, and I don't even think she had heard that phrase until that night, when she sat down to watch the story about Joe's life.

Dylan and Maelyn sat down to watch.

And with each passing second, Dylan's excitement turned to sadness. They heard Sharri talk about Joe: "I just knew I wanted to have children with him, grow old with him . . ."

They saw the footage of the planes hitting the towers.

With every passing second, Dylan's smile disappeared a little more and a little more.

They heard Sharri say, "It took a part of me, and that part can't be replaced. It's just gone."

By the time the story ended, Dylan and Maelyn were bawling and hugging each other.

Dylan was overwhelmed by it. She couldn't understand. All of a sudden, she was filled with questions for us. She thought about the kind of person who would hijack a plane and fly it into a building, and she said, "He had to be drunk. He was drunk, right?" She had heard of drunk drivers. That was where her mind went, to a poor decision instead of calculated intent to murder.

We tried to explain. "Sometimes bad people do bad things."

It's hard to know exactly how much to tell a seven-year-old. It's hard to explain the unexplainable.

And then, as we talked, we started to explain how this all connected to her family. We told her that sometimes people do bad things, but good can come out of it, too. We told her what she would have figured out herself, eventually. "If 9/11 hadn't happened, you wouldn't be here."

To which Dylan replied, "Why couldn't Mom just have had me with Joe?"

Every year on September 11, Cantor Fitzgerald holds two events. One is a 9/11 service. My mother goes every year, to support the Esposito family. She listens to them read the names of the people who worked at Cantor Fitzgerald.

The other event is called Charity Day. Essentially, all the company's salaries and commissions from the day goes to charities. Celebrities come in, take calls, and execute trades. Then the money goes to the charity they are representing. Edie Lutnick, who lost her brother Gary in the attacks, runs Charity Day. Edie's other brother, Howard, is now the chairman and CEO of Cantor Fitzgerald.

In 2014, I was one of the people asked to attend. I was there on behalf of A Caring Hand: The Billy Esposito Foundation and Tuesday's Children, which provides personalized support to traumatized, grief-stricken children and families who are reeling from terrorism or traumatic loss.

I brought Devon with me.

Cantor Fitzgerald had moved its offices to midtown, on Fifty-ninth Street between Park and Lexington Avenues. We bumped into Craig Esposito on our way in.

I really didn't know what to expect, but when the whole Esposito family had arrived, we went in, and I realized it was a huge event. The celebrities included Julianne Moore, Billy Crystal, Whoopi Goldberg, Rudy Giuliani, Billie Jean King, and David Blaine. Cantor Fitzgerald would raise $12 million for charities that day. On the way out, as we were leaving, we even got to meet Jamie Foxx, which Devon thought was pretty cool, and so did I. He told us how big a fan he was of the Dallas Cowboys.

While we were on the trading floor, I walked around introducing Devon to as many people as I could. "This is Joe Maio's son." One of the people he got to meet was Cantor Fitzgerald's CEO, Howard Lutnick. The two stood off to the side for a few minutes, Lutnick talking to another Maio. I stared at them and wondered how often Joe got to speak to Lutnick. I overheard a part of the conversation.

Howard told Devon, "Your father was a great man."

I got worked up hearing that. My eyes were welling up. Teardrops dripped down my face, but when I looked over at Devon, he wasn't crying. He didn't show much emotion at all. But I was happy he got a chance to see where his dad would have worked—even though it was a different office, it was still Cantor Fitzgerald, and Howard Lutnick was still the boss, and it gave us a small window into Joe's everyday life. Devon didn't talk about any of this. He sat mostly silent on the car ride home. When we got home, the flowers I had ordered for his mom had been delivered. I buy her flowers every year on September 11.

The anniversary of 9/11 is, of course, a very solemn day for our country. It's a national day of remembrance. All these years later, and it's still hard to comprehend such massive, senseless violence.

But for Sharri, it's very personal. I think whenever you lose a loved one, especially at a young age, the date is engraved in your mind forever.

And generally, if you lost a family member on 9/11, your friends and even a lot of acquaintances are conscious of it. If someone dies from cancer, only a few people will remember the date it happened. If you lost a loved one on 9/11, then a lot of people in your social circle will think of you on September 11 every year.

In some ways, this can be comforting—you don't get the sense that the rest of the world has forgotten your family member—which can happen if, for example, your lost some-body to cancer—but it creates a weird dynamic.

One year, on 9/11, I went to the gym in the morning, then walked back into the house. Sharri was sitting in the living room, just there staring at the TV as they scrolled through the names of everybody who died. And as I walked in, the name JOE MAIO scrolled onto the screen. I mean, almost *immediately*. It was like somebody timed it for me to walk in as soon as his name came up, like a scene in a movie.

It's hard to imagine being reminded about the worst day of your life every single year so publicly.

I understand why we do it. I've been a member of the me-dia for most of my adult life. I get it. I understand part of our job is to commemorate things—to look back at anniversaries of important moments. D-day. When JFK was shot. 9/11. If a major media outlet ignored the anniversary, people would go crazy.

But it's difficult. Every year this comes up, and it's like the whole country is asking Sharri to relive this. She can't just do it privately in whatever way feels right for her.

And really, when people say, "9/11," I say, "Really, it's the whole week and month leading up to it." Once you get past Labor Day, it just sets in on you. It's the end of summer, the start of school, and the start of football season, which is a big-ger deal to me than to most people. Everything is a reminder of what time of year it is.

September days in New York are so great—the weather is just perfect. September 11, 2001, was such a beautiful day. It was a spectacular late-summer day in New York—there is really no better match of weather and location than September in New York City.

The sun was out, and the sky was clear. It was sixty-eight degrees in Central Park when the first plane hit the World Trade Center. I mean, if you were in a climate-controlled room, that's the temperature you would choose.

I think that's one small reason the tragedy was so jarring for people—it was one of those peaceful, perfect September days when you just feel so happy to be alive, and then somebody chose to commit these unspeakable acts. It's obviously not the main reason why it resonated with the whole country, but it's somewhere down on the list. You see it in novels, when writers use the weather to give you a sense of how people feel that day. Even today, when there is perfect autumn weather in New York, you will hear New Yorkers call them "9/11 days." That's how we think of them. *9/11 days.*

So it creeps up on us, inexorably. The calendar flips to September, and we think, *Here it comes.* There's no recipe or formula for navigating that. You just have to do it. I'm no better at it than anybody else. I just try to be a kind, sympathetic, understanding person. That's all it is. I just have to be conscious of it and sensitive to it. However Sharri feels is OK. Whatever she needs to do, she should do. It's a painful time of year, and I try to treat it that way. The right thing to do is just to try to do the right thing. Sometimes Sharri still thinks of the day itself, and it's so suffocating that she has to force herself to breathe.

Grief can make you a casualty, and fear can make you a prisoner. Sharri's strength helped her build a new life for herself and for Devon after Joe died, but she still had her fear of flying. I understood it and worked around it. When I decided to take Dylan on a Disney cruise, I asked my mother to come with me because I knew Sharri would not.

But then, after many years, Sharri confronted her fear. She decided she did not want to be a person who spent her whole life within driving distance of her house. And she did not want Devon and Dylan to be afraid of flying.

The first time she got on a plane with the kids, and without me, was in March 2016. That was the day of the terrorist attack in Brussels. She didn't want to get on the plane, but she didn't want to cancel. She got through it.

The more she flew, the easier it got for her, but she still gets anxious on planes. In 2017, she flew to Colorado, Florida, Arizona, California, Massachusetts, and Michigan—all in one year. That was impressive for her. The only real problem was when we went to Florida. I had purchased plane tickets for Adam Schefter, Dylan Schefter, Devon Maio, and Sharri Schefter. But Sharri's license says Sharri Maio.

So as soon as we went through security, TSA agents pulled her over and treated her as if she had broken the law. They pulled her aside for about twenty minutes. They patted her down. They found her diabetes pump and wanted to know what it was. I stood with Devon and Dylan and watched in horror. Devon kept saying, "Mom is going to be so mad at you"—all for booking her a plane ticket under the wrong name, a mistake I never will make again.

For a while, we thought she wouldn't be allowed on the plane. And Devon was right; she was furious at me. How about that irony? After all these years of being scared to get on a plane, she was mad because somebody wouldn't let her get on one. Eventually, she was able to board, and we flew to Florida, looking every bit like a conventional American family of four.

I have taken Devon and Dylan back to Bellmore, where I grew up, to some of the places I used to go: Bagel City (now called Town Bagel), down on Merrick Road, and Hunan Gourmet, where I worked as a busboy in high school, making sixty or seventy bucks a night in cash tips, plus a plate of chicken and broccoli with a Coke at the end of the night. Man, did I look forward to that meal. Hunan Gourmet isn't there anymore—it has been replaced by another store—but to me, that still is the place where my work ethic formed. I wanted them to see the spot.

If Joe had lived, he would probably take Devon—and more kids, if he and Sharri had had them—to north Jersey, where he grew up. And then they would drive around, and Joe Maio would tell Joe Maio stories.

He would take Devon to the house where he grew up. He would explain that his family was one of the first in the neighborhood to have a finished walk-out basement with a wet bar. He would host little Intellivision tournaments for his buddies. Maybe he would tell them about the pool party when his parents were out of town.

He would say that when he was a boy, he would stack Chips Ahoy! cookies inside a glass, fill the glass with milk to the top, crush the cookies, and eat the concoction with a spoon.

He would tell Devon about Waffles. Waffles was the Maios' dog; when guests came, he would growl and hide under beds and really just wasn't very nice. Joe would tell Devon that one time, his friend Cory Tovin said, "He's just growling. He's not really that mean." Cory said he would put his hand under the bed.

Joe said, "Cory, don't put your hand under there. He will bite you." Cory stuck his foot under the bed instead. Moments later, the sock was gone, and Cory had a puncture wound in his foot.

Joe would laugh.

He would say Cory became one of his college roommates, and he remained one of his best friends until he moved down to Atlanta, and they don't talk as much as they should. Joe would make a mental note to give Cory a call, see how he was doing.

He would tell Devon that he hoped he enjoyed being a kid as much as Joe did. He'd had a good childhood—a little wild at times, as most good childhoods are. He had an acute sense of wonder. He would find a rock or piece of plastic on the beach and think it was a treasure. He always seemed to find something and run to his mom and dad to show them what he found.

Joe would show Devon where he rode his BMX dirt bike during the day and where he rode snowmobiles at night. He would see that the rink in Montvale where he used to roller-skate is gone now, but he would show Devon the pond off Hungry Hollow Road where he used to play ice hockey.

He would not say that when he was a boy, all his peers wanted to be friends with him, and a lot of them wanted to *be* him. He was not the type to flaunt his popularity.

Maybe Devon would figure that out about his father.

Maybe Anthony would be with them, to explain.

Joe would take Devon to one of his favorite old pizza places, DaVinci's, and laugh at their "thin crust gourmet pizza," which DaVinci's promised "is an incredibly guilt-free way to get your 'carb' fix." Back in Joe's day, you got your slice, and maybe you put some parmesan cheese or garlic or red pepper on it, and that was that.

Maybe he would point across the street to where he used to order a beer at Silo before he was old enough to legally do it, because he knew the owner.

And he would take Devon to that overpass on Scotland Hill Road, the one that terrified him as a kid because he was scared of heights. *Isn't that strange?* Joe would say. *And I ended up working in one of the tallest buildings in America.*

19

I spent the last weekend before 9/11 in New York. It was the opening weekend of the NFL season, but the team I covered, the Broncos, did not play until Monday night, September 10. I decided to visit my family on Long Island.

The night before I left Denver, I went on a date with a woman named Annie. It went well—so well that I did not sleep much that night. My mind was racing. I went through my usual emotional cycle: *Hopes are up; this is the one; let's hit fast-forward.* Before I showered, dressed, and packed the next morning, I was up at 5:45 A.M., talking to my mom on the phone about Annie.

That relationship with Annie would fade, like all my others, but I didn't know that at the time. I thought Annie might be the one. Then again, at various times I convinced myself a hundred women might be the one.

My mom picked me up at the airport with Marni's three-year-old son, Casey, in the back seat. He was wearing blue sunglasses and looked adorable. We met up with my family for dinner in Wantagh to celebrate Poppy Dave's eightieth birthday.

My weekend in New York was filled with people from my past but also with hints that I had an empty future. I went for a four-mile run with my dad, the same path that we always ran, from our house on Judith Drive, up to Merrick Road, and back. I ate at Bagel City, my favorite bagel place, where I loved plain bagels with whitefish salad. My mom and I took Casey and his younger sister, Sydney, to *Sesame Street Live!* at Nassau Coliseum, where I saw all the parents with all their kids and was reminded of what I was missing.

I was only thirty-four, but my urge to find a wife never left my mind. My desire to meet the perfect woman was always foolish, but it was becoming more foolish as I got older. When you hit your midthirties, you have to accept that any woman you date might have kids, but that possibility made me squeamish. You don't read many fairy tales that start with "She left her two daughters from a previous marriage with a babysitter for the evening and . . ."

I wanted a résumé without blemishes. That meant no kids. I wanted to start from scratch.

Part of falling in love is finding the right person, but part of it is when you find them. You can't just *want* to meet somebody; you have to be capable of making a relationship work. You have to be in the right frame of mind.

As I look back, I realize that for a long time I wasn't capable. It didn't matter who I dated. No relationship would have lasted very long. I would have botched it. I was so sure I was ready for marriage and everything that came with it, and I just wasn't there, and I don't know that anybody would have gotten me there. I even blamed Denver, the city where I'd had so many dating failures, but no city would have gotten me there. When you know something is wrong, it's easy to look around and try to figure out what it is, but what I saw was the city and these women. I never saw me.

The older you get, the more your guard drops, and the more open-minded you become, and the more you learn and grow, until you meet somebody at the right time who is a special person, and it works at that time in your life.

I look back at it now and I realize I was looking for a boost from somebody else, but nobody should derive their happiness entirely from somebody else. It just doesn't work. You can't begin a relationship by placing that kind of burden on another person, but at the time, I couldn't see it. All I could see was my dating failures and my dreams.

We arrived at Nassau Coliseum. When we walked in, I saw a woman I'd had a crush on at Michigan. I ran into a good high school friend, met his wife, and wondered why I couldn't find somebody like that. I described her in my journal:

The type of woman I would have loved to meet . . .
but that world is so different than mine. Family
oriented, big groups. I'm out here in Denver by
myself, all alone. Big difference.

I immersed myself in football, first by watching Michigan lose at Washington, then by going online to see if there was anything new on the Broncos front. I found that they had signed running back Mike Anderson to a four-year deal, to my surprise. Work stress briefly replaced personal stress. Then I went back to personal stress.

I saw my friend David Simon's dad, Arnie, and he said I looked like I had the weight of the world on my shoulders. I did. I was anxious to find the right woman for me.

Just about anyone can pick up on it, I'll bet, I wrote in my journal.

I went home and fell into my usual routine. I watched football, knowing I should pull myself away from it but unable to do so. I called Annie. I wrote a story. I wondered why Annie hadn't called back. I paid a bill and made some work calls. I wondered again why Annie hadn't called back. I tossed and turned that night.

The next day was a highly anticipated one in Denver. The Broncos were opening their new stadium, then called Invesco Field at Mile High, against the defending NFC champion Giants. It was a big moment for that football-crazed town, and the atmosphere was electric. Nine retired Broncos legends walked on the field before the game, linking the past to the present. If you are a sports fan at all, you understand why that was a really cool moment.

The Broncos won, but the enduring memory of the game was of violence: Wide receiver Ed McCaffrey, one of the most popular players in the city, broke his leg. It was one of those gruesome injuries that casts a pall over the rest of the game. Ed would never be the same player again.

While I was in the press box, Annie called back. I was mostly annoyed that it had taken her so long—not excited that she had called back. She did not want to hit fast-forward like I did.

After the game, I drove my friend Thomas George of *The New York Times* back to the Renaissance Hotel by the old Stapleton Airport. It was 12:30 A.M. Mountain Time on September 11, 2001.

Thomas was a longtime friend and mentor. He, more than anyone, was responsible for me pursuing a career in journalism. Back when I was working for *The Michigan Daily*, Thomas was a sports reporter for *The Detroit Free Press*, covering multiple Michigan sporting events. He was kind enough to take me under his wing, guide me, influence me, and convince me that I could make a living as a reporter, which was something I never before realized. Thomas and I got closer over the years, and he had gone from helping me professionally to helping me personally. He asked me about my dating life. I told him about Annie. I said I had called her the day before, and she took more than a day to call me back. It really bothered me.

Thomas gave me some advice. He said I had to accept that not everybody was as punctual as I was. He told me I couldn't carry past relationships into future ones. He said I needed to keep an open mind.

He said, "People bring their baggage to the Lord, and then they bring it back with them. They need to leave it there."

Sound advice, I wrote in my journal, and I climbed into bed in Denver feeling buoyed by what he'd said.

In a house on Long Island, Joe Maio was asleep next to his wife. He had less than eight hours to live.

20

On the morning Joe Maio died, he was supposed to drive to Connecticut with one of his coworkers at Cantor Fitzgerald, Keith Coleman. They had a meeting there that afternoon. Joe had three options:

1. Stay home that morning, then go straight to Connecticut for the meeting.
2. Drive straight to Connecticut and work there all morning before the meeting.
3. Go to his office in the World Trade Center in the morning, then go to Connecticut in the afternoon.

He chose number three.

He still had to figure out *how* he would get to the World Trade Center before heading up to Connecticut. Joe usually drove to work, but on this day, he did not want to drive there, then drive to Connecticut, and then drive home afterward.

That was too much driving. He decided to take a ferry to Manhattan, a train or car service to Connecticut for the meeting, and then a car service home from Connecticut that night.

Now he had one more decision: How should he get to the ferry stop? He did not want to leave his car there, because he would not be taking the ferry home that night.

So he asked his wife to drive him to the ferry early that morning.

Sharri was annoyed. She thought about Devon.

You want me to wake up a fourteen-month-old at 6:00 in the morning to take you to the ferry?

They argued about it. Joe won. Sharri woke up, piled Devon and their dog, Riley, in the car, and drove Joe to the ferry for the first and only time. They never had done that before, not until this 9/11 morning. By the time they got to the ferry, the argument had faded away.

"I love you," she told Joe.

She kissed him goodbye, forever.

What if Joe Maio had stayed home that morning?

He would have lived, presumably for several decades. Devon would know his father. I never would have met Sharri. Dylan would not be here. One seemingly mundane decision ended this great man's life and altered so many more.

I am fascinated by it. Sharri is not.

She thinks Joe died tragically for the same reason that Keith Coleman died tragically. Sharri says, "Joe was supposed to be at work that morning. That's where he was supposed to be."

She was always attracted to hardworking men. Joe Maio was one until the end.

This is how Sharri has lived her post-Joe life. She doesn't play the what-if game; she doesn't wonder how small decisions led to his death. She also doesn't go to the other extreme, like some people do: telling herself that Joe was not only supposed to work but he was supposed to die that day.

A few years ago, at a baby shower, Sharri was talking to a deeply religious woman who had also lost her husband on 9/11. The woman said that God wanted three thousand people in heaven. Sharri thought, *What?* People can grieve or cope in whatever way works for them, but Sharri could not understand how somebody could say any death on 9/11 was "meant to be." She has a clear-eyed view of how he died: He was living his life, and terrorists took it away from him.

Sharri does not believe in fate. I do—to an extent. I believe in it more than Sharri does. I certainly don't believe Joe's death was "meant to be" or that Sharri was fated to be a 9/11 widow and then meet me. But I do think that *after* she became a 9/11 widow, she was supposed to meet me. That's what I want to believe.

Thousands of people died on 9/11. All are missed, but none were perfect. The more I learned about Joe Maio, though, the more impressed I was. I could tell people were not just saying nice things because he had died young. They would have said the same if he had lived. He was a golden boy. He was enormously successful but didn't flaunt it. Women loved him, and men understood why.

I had always heard about finding the One, and I never knew how people knew. Were there signs from above? Did lights flash? When I heard that Joe and I had the same birthday, I liked that. It was this little hint that Sharri and I were supposed to be together. It was a nudge. You can't build a lifelong relationship on a nudge, but it's a nice start.

And as I continued dating Sharri, and as I heard so much about Joe, I thought, *If she was good enough for Joe Maio, she was good enough for me.* I know that sounds crazy, leaning on a man you never even met, but I had that thought, more than once, before I decided to propose to Sharri. It affirmed my beliefs. It was almost like taking a test when you already know the answers. I knew I could do it.

I feel honored to be married to the woman who was married to Joe Maio.

George thinks of it in his own way. He says that he feels like Joe sent me.

Joe is buried next to Anthony at St. Anthony's Catholic Cemetery in Nanuet, New York. George goes to the cemetery sometimes. Paula can't bring herself to do it. Sharri has not gone there at all since Anthony died.

Sharri never has visited the 9/11 memorial and has no intention of going. She has no desire to go. It doesn't matter how tasteful or beautiful or moving it is—to Sharri, that's just the place where she lost Joe, and going back there would bring her back to the most devastating moment in her life. She sees the new World Trade Center building and thinks, *Who wants to rent space there?*

She does not need any reminders that he died; she lives with that every day. It is her reality. Over time, the pain gets less acute. Living gets easier. But the reality does not change. The scar tissue does not go away and never will.

In the summer of 2017, Devon did an internship with

CNBC's Jim Cramer, who founded TheStreet, a financial news-and-analysis site. Devon has a real passion for business. I was hoping this would inspire him toward a career he loves.

I took him into Manhattan on the first day of his internship to show him how to get to the office by train. Devon may look back on it as the first commute of a life full of them. We got on a crowded 7:27 A.M. train—for a while, we weren't able to sit together because it was so busy and all the seats were taken—and went into Penn Station. Then we took the No. 3 subway downtown. I took pictures of Devon on the subway, which is a very dad thing to do. We asked strangers on the subway about the stops where we might get off, and they were kind and helpful. I wanted Devon to feel like he knew exactly what to do the next day when he went to work in New York City on his own.

Eventually our stop came. We got off at Wall Street. As we walked along that particular subway stop, we looked up and saw all kinds of signs for the 9/11 museum and Wall Street. They were signs to him but reminders to us. Devon's desk was across the street from the New York Stock Exchange.

Devon didn't say anything. He doesn't talk about this stuff. But it felt to me like the spirit of Joe was watching over him.

Devon says he is not ready to visit the 9/11 memorial, but sometimes he opens the large boxes that Sharri saved for him, full of letters to Devon from Joe's friends, telling him stories about his father. Joe's friends sent those letters for Devon to read one day so he could know the type of man Joe was. The box holds the plastic Cantor Fitzgerald ID that was found after Joe died.

As he gets older, Devon may have more questions. What would his father tell him? What advice would he give? How would he console him, lift him up, or set him straight? Maybe it will all click for Devon if he becomes a father, and the words that George uttered to Joe will echo for Devon:

"You don't know what love is until you have your own child."

Joe has not faded from our lives. He lives on, through Devon, through Sharri, and even through Dylan and me. His presence is constant. He is the fifth member of our family, never seen but always there. Every morning, I wake up knowing that at some point that day, my wife will think about another man she still loves. When we watch a movie from a decade or two ago, Sharri always checks the release date to see if Joe was alive when it came out.

As Sharri got ready for our latest renovation, she realized that in order to do it, the mural with the flowers and green grass and blue skies would have to be destroyed.

She had commissioned it in 2001, while Joe was alive, and watched the painter work on it during her darkest days. It had helped sustain her. Now it was 2017, and she watched as construction workers took the Sheetrock with the mural on it, piece by piece, to a dumpster.

She was surprised to discover she was OK with it. She no longer needed the brightness that the mural once provided. As the years passed, the mural came to remind her more of that time in her life when she was in such pain because she'd lost Joe. She would rather remember his life than his death. Even today, when Sharri redecorates a room, she sometimes pulls out an old picture of Joe that was in storage and puts it on a shelf.

Two months before he died, Joe Maio moved into a new house.

Joe never knew me, but here I am, living his life. I occupy

his space. I fall asleep next to his wife and have helped raise his son. I call his parents on his birthday.

I have lived in that house for almost twelve years now—far longer than Joe did. But every time I come home, I feel like I'm walking into Joe Maio's house. And I am.

Afterword

From the moment this book was conceived, I had conflicting emotions about it. The story meant everything to me, but I wasn't sure why anybody else would want to read it. I wanted to honor Joe, but did not want to relive the hardest days of my life. I wanted Adam to use his platform to help remind people of all the lives that were lost and altered on 9/11, but I don't personally enjoy that kind of attention. I was not sure I wanted Adam to write the book at all, but if he did, I wanted him to be completely honest.

I helped Adam the best I could. But I could not bring myself to read the book until just a few weeks before publication. Reading it was painful, but also cathartic.

Now, as the paperback version is being released, I can say that I'm glad my husband wrote the book, and I am appreciative of the positive reaction, even if I don't fully understand some of it.

It took me by surprise when random people who know Adam came up to me and said, "Oh, I loved the book," or "I can relate to that." I did not think of our lives as relatable. I just thought of them as ours. But a lot of people said, "I could relate to that situation, the blending of families, having to raise somebody else's child."

I got a call out of the blue from one of Joe's coworkers from Cantor Fitzgerald. He was in Tokyo the same time we were there, and he went to our wedding. He said he loved the book, and he said he married somebody who had children, and it felt like a very similar situation.

Some people said they found it "inspirational." I thought: *inspirational?* It's just our lives. I know that nothing I did was inspirational. I think that if you or anybody else were in my place, God forbid, or any tough situation like it, and you had kids, you would keep going. That's all I did after Joe died: I kept going, for Devon's sake. I couldn't imagine giving up. Devon gave me a purpose.

A year down the road, two years down the road, I got a sense there might be another life for me, another chance to be happy again.

And then my knight in shining armor came along . . . in his orange shirt.

(I wonder if he still has that shirt somewhere. I'm afraid to look!)

Thankfully, compared to the general population, very few people have gone through what I went through. But almost everybody goes through a really hard time. I think people could relate because we're just normal people trying to figure it out as we go.

Adam kept his promise of being honest. He wrote about his dating difficulties, the times he was lonely, and his struggle to blend into our lives—which was more of a struggle in his mind than in mine or Devon's.

People came to me and said, "Wow, Adam really put it out there. I don't know if I could do that." To me, that's just Adam. If he wasn't going to be honest, why bother writing the book at all?

We had nothing to hide. This is our story.

Thank you for reading.

Sharri Maio

Acknowledgments

Thank you to everybody who shared personal anecdotes and thoughts and who helped fill in the gaps in our story, including Paula and George Maio, Little Joe Maio, JoAnn and Chuck Setty, Robyn and Jordan Goldman, Shirley and Jeffrey Schefter, Marni and Mike Barone, Jordan Schefter, Jordan Bergstein, Casey Cummings, Craig Esposito, Susie Esposito, Stevie Esposito, Adam Gordon, Jeff Heitzner, Jeff Moallem, Kim Rothofsky, Jeff and Stefanie Rubin, Lori Sloves, Duane Tarrant, and Cory Tovin.

A big thank-you to the team at Creative Artists Agency—especially Dave Larabell, Nick Khan, and David Koonin—for pushing this project into a reality. Without them, this story would have been shared only within our family. ESPN first brought it to light when coordinating producer Greg Jewell and producer Dominique Collins turned our story into an ESPN feature that ran on the fifteenth anniversary of 9/11; they turned an idea into a tasteful feature that honored Joe's memory.

Thank you to Marc Resnick and the team at St. Martin's

Press for believing in this book from the beginning. And a huge thank-you and debt of gratitude to another Michigan Man and master wordsmith, Michael Rosenberg, for bringing all the words and all the stories from all these people together in a way only he could.

Joe Maio

1. For two men who never met, Joe and Adam have a lot in common, beyond marrying the same woman. Why do you think Adam wanted to write a book about Joe?

2. How did the way Joe lived his life inform the reaction to his death?

3. Sharri shows incredible poise at Joe's memorial service. What does that tell us about how she has lived in the ensuing years? What would you do if you were in Sharri's position right after 9/11? Would you want to take any method of transportation, or even leave the house?

4. How did Joe's death affect Anthony, Joe's parents, and Sharri in different ways? Have you lost a family member? What helps to survive such a deep loss?

5. Although the story is largely intended as a salute to Joe, Adam opens up about his own failures and vulnerabilities. How does this add to the story? What kind of example does this set for Devon?

6. How did Adam's previous dating failures affect his courtship of Sharri? How did Joe's death affect Sharri's approach to dating, once she was ready to date again?

7. When Anthony took his own life, Adam's initial reaction was anger. What does that say about Adam's connection to Joe, and his fatherly protectiveness of Devon?

8. How has Devon helped George and Paula deal with tragedy?

9. Why do you think Sharri keeps redecorating her house?

10. What does Joe's relationship with Adam Gordon tell us about Joe?

11. In what ways is Joe's presence still felt?

12. What does it mean when Sharri removes the mural at the end of the book?

Adam Schefter is one of the most influential voices in football today. He is ubiquitous across all of ESPN's platforms—TV, radio, and digital. He has the largest Twitter following of any personality in football. He lives in New York with his wife, Sharri; son, Devon; and daughter, Dylan.

Michael Rosenberg is a senior writer at *Sports Illustrated* and author of the critically acclaimed *War As They Knew It*. Most recently he is the collaborator on Joe Buck's memoir, *Lucky Bastard*.